The African American Missional Pastor

The African American Missional Pastor

Effecting Social Change Through the Power of Embodied Preaching in Florida

By
MELVIN L. MONTGOMERY JR.

Foreword by Anna M. Droll

WIPF & STOCK · Eugene, Oregon

THE AFRICAN AMERICAN MISSIONAL PASTOR
Effecting Social Change Through the Power of Embodied Preaching in Florida

Copyright © 2026 Melvin L. Montgomery Jr. All rights reserved. Except for brief quotations in critical publications or reviews, no part of this book may be reproduced in any manner without prior written permission from the publisher. Write: Permissions, Wipf and Stock Publishers, 199 W. 8th Ave., Suite 3, Eugene, OR 97401.

Wipf & Stock
An Imprint of Wipf and Stock Publishers
199 W. 8th Ave., Suite 3
Eugene, OR 97401

www.wipfandstock.com

PAPERBACK ISBN: 979-8-3852-2877-5
HARDCOVER ISBN: 979-8-3852-2878-2
EBOOK ISBN: 979-8-3852-2879-9

VERSION NUMBER 020226

Scripture quotations marked (ESV) are taken from The ESV® Bible (The Holy Bible, English Standard Version®), © 2001 by Crossway, a publishing ministry of Good News Publishers. Used by permission. All rights reserved.

Scripture quotations marked (NET) are taken from the NET Bible® copyright ©1996–2017 All rights reserved. Build 30170414 by Biblical Studies Press, L.L.C.

Scripture quotations marked (NRSV) are from the New Revised Standard Version Bible, copyright © 1989 National Council of the Churches of Christ in the United States of America. Used by permission. All rights reserved worldwide.

CONTENTS

ACKNOWLEDGMENTS

THE COMPLETION OF THIS project could not have been possible without the guidance and expertise of my dissertation advisor, Professor Dr. Anna Droll, PhD. I would also like to thank Dr. Droll for encouraging me to pursue this topic. I would like to thank each church leader for participating in this research and providing their insights and perspectives. Their participation is critical to this project.

Lastly, to my parents, Melvin L. Montgomery Sr. and Earmie L. Hughes, I owe a debt of gratitude for motivating and encouraging me to complete this project and for their support throughout my doctoral journey. I want to thank my wife, Toyka, for always being there for me and helping proofread my papers. Special thanks go to my daughters, Norsha and Ashelyn Montgomery, for their love and support. I would also like to thank my mother-in-law, Eliza Campbell, and my aunts, Jean and Martha Campbell, who went out of their way to assist me in whatever way possible. I thank my classmates and cohort for their helpful discussions and good ideas throughout this journey. I am forever thankful.

In addition, I want to pay a very special tribute to the memory of my precious grandmother, Mrs. Beatrice Patterson, my stepdad, Deacon Charles L. Hughes Sr., and my grandmother by marriage, Mrs. Ella Mae Campbell, without whose spiritual blessing I would not have been able to complete my doctoral dissertation.

FOREWORD

All eyes are on Minnesota at the time of the writing of this foreword on behalf of Dr. Melvin Montgomery. The churches of America are in full view of the suffering and sorrow arising from the streets of Minneapolis at the hands of unbridled and brutal government sanctioned force. This is a sorrow that shares a profound kinship with the suffering that often accompanies living black in the United States, and therefore Montgomery's book holds immense significance for all readers. In fact, it launches like an arrow at the target of systemic injustice and serves as a reminder that the energies that compel what we see today have always been present with us. Today we are just seeing a grotesque elaboration of the will to exclude, terrorize, and eradicate the "other."

Montgomery allows us to release our preoccupation with the streets of Minnesota long enough to consider the streets, pulpits, and boardrooms of Florida where brave men and women practiced and still practice their Christian faith in the public sphere on behalf of the community at large. What Montgomery shares brings hope! He sets center stage the stories of those who have lifted their voices and placed their bodies on the line in their own eras. Therefore, the will to exclude and diminish finds its robust contender, in Montgomery's work, as the will to advocate for inclusion and flourishing and justice for all. What he does is amplify this life-giving rebuttal, but only after he sets the contexts, both past and present, for the evil of racism, after he acknowledges the challenges being faced by the church, and after he admonishes the lack of courage in those in the church who *should* be appropriating their influence for the sake of social justice.

Furthermore, the implications of what Montgomery brings is hugely important for theology. His emphasis on embodied preaching can only sound a clarion theological critique of an evangelical Christian theology that dismisses emphasis on social responsibility as a biblically grounded, theological imperative. Montgomery calls out certain *practitioners* of theology, the pastors that omit the obvious in their sermons and seem to disconnect with the needs on the streets. As well, he highlights theologies that, on the other hand, have found their very impetus embedded in the streets. For example, context has been essential for Howard Thurman, James Cone, and many others in the construction of a black theology that cares for the bodies and souls of African Americans, those on the street. Yet, I am hopeful that Montgomery's work might reverberate beyond to alert those brands of evangelical theology that reflect little on theology as practice.

Decades ago, theologian Paul Tillich had suggested that theology, "before theology tells its message," can ask "what is most important to the people being addressed." Millard Erickson picked up the idea to write, "The doctrine of humanity is one point where it is possible to get a toehold in the mind of the modern secular person. For it at least begins with topics that are on the mind of the person in the street."[1] In other words, the idea is that theology can be done in a dialogical way, starting first from the point of inquiry arising from the secular world. When done that way, whether with the "unchurched" or the "churched," the doctrine of humanity and the doctrine of the image of God in humankind lead, or *should* lead, seamlessly to emphasis on social responsibility and Christian duty. What Montgomery is saying is that it is crucial for the church to reflect on what theological questions may be arising from the streets, whether of Minneapolis or of Florida. "Does God care?" "Does the church care?"

1. Erickson, *Christian Theology*, 426, 427.

These are the questions arising from the crushed hearts of the brutalized and their onlookers. In Montgomery's book, we find answers to both of them.

Anna M. Droll
Pompano Beach, Florida,
January 2026

CHAPTER ONE

INTRODUCTION

THIS BOOK BEGINS WITH the assumption that those who preach matter, and African American preaching matters, particularly in Florida. Preaching is a significant aspect of African American religious and cultural heritage. Florida has a rich history of African American preaching rooted in slavery. Moreover, the African American preaching tradition has advocated for social justice throughout its long history, mainly during the era of the Civil Rights Movement. However, is the risk of preaching on social justice issues perceived too great in our contemporary context? This book examines how African Americans employed "embodied" preaching in Florida to address social justice issues. It also examines how African American justice preachers today continue in the practice of living their lives as embodied sermons.

African American preachers' preaching style and content have been profoundly shaped by lived experience under the hegemony of white dominance—marked by oppression, discrimination, and a resilient faith in God. In the 1983 Lyman Beecher Lectures at Yale Divinity School, Kelly Miller Smith insists that social crisis preaching is not optional commentary but an essential dimension of Christian proclamation. Smith argues that "preaching is no mere human undertaking. . . . It is a divine-human enterprise and is properly concerned with the whole of life," thereby grounding proclamation in both theological depth and lived reality.[1] He further clarifies that social crisis preaching is not reducible to moral commentary or political rhetoric, stating that "the concern is with the proclamation of that which is crucially relevant within the context of the Christian gospel in times that are critical in terms of social dynamics and machinations."[2] Consequently, any preaching that ignores concrete social realities forfeits its integrity, for, as Smith forcefully concludes, "concern with social crises is not simply permissible in preaching; it is imperative. . . . Without it preaching is weak and anemic and is hardly worth the name."[3]

Social justice is a concept that promotes equality among every member of our society, regardless of race, ethnicity, gender, or education, and encourages offering equal opportunities, privileges, community resources, and protections under the law to all. The term *social justice*, which demands fairness for all people, can be troublesome to some. Social justice preaching speaks out against injustice, targeting specific political or social issues like the societal dangers of driving while black and brown and the blatant unfair treatment of African Americans by the United States justice system. Embodied social justice preaching is the active engagement in pursuing social justice enacted by preachers.

Social justice preaching aims to create a culture of generosity and equality. I know that the African American pulpit has long been the center of the African American community, and the voice of the African American pastor/preacher has been esteemed for his/her consistent cry for justice and equality within this country. Growing up in Gary, Indiana, in a black Baptist church setting, the magnetic voices of black preachers have been a dominant soundtrack of my life. From my youth, black pastors and preachers' impassioned sermons were not just rituals to sit through but were riveting tales of resilience, resistance, and hope that made my heart race and inflamed in me a passion for preaching.

1. Smith, *Social Crisis Preaching*, 18.
2. Smith, *Social Crisis Preaching*, 18.
3. Smith, *Social Crisis Preaching*, 18.

I felt what James Earl Massey calls the *burdensome joy of preaching*.[4] Dr. Massey was dean emeritus and Distinguished Professor-at-Large at the Anderson University School of Theology in Anderson, Indiana. He was the former senior pastor of Detroit's Metropolitan Church and former dean of the chapel at Tuskegee University in Tuskegee, Alabama. "Massey begins by dealing with the inward side of preaching. Preaching is audacious because it presumes to speak for God. It makes sense, then, that a sense of calling would be paramount."[5] Massey explains that the black preacher must be able to tell "The Story." The Story immediately recalls one or more of the three levels to which African American believers are sensitive in our contact with Scripture: "(1) the events reported there as happenings; (2) the canonical interpretation of those events; and (3) the divine action associated with the reported happenings."[6] Massey goes on to say that "the Christian preacher is the steward of The Story, a person entrusted to administer biblical truth as a steward of God and the Father of Jesus Christ, as agent intent and eager to see the consequences of that telling effected in personal and social history."[7]

In our community, the church was not just a place of worship but a refuge. It was a place where black people congregated to share stories of joys and sorrows and to feel and express the love of Christ. However, more than that, the black church was inspirational, a place where injustice was confronted head-on. The black church was also a place to muster the courage to confront and examine our assumptions and presuppositions. It was where we could interrogate our prejudices and prejudgments. That evaluation is what Socrates meant in Plato's *Apology*: "The unexamined life is not worth living."[8]

Through the lens of black preaching, I learned *paideia*. *Paideia* is a Greek word that means "training of the physical and

4. After his book by the same name.
5. Preaching.com, "Burdensome Joy of Preaching."
6. Massey, *Stewards of the Story*, xv.
7. Massey, *Stewards of the Story*, xv.
8. Plato, *Apology* 38 (Jowett).

mental faculties in such a way as to produce a broad, enlightened, mature outlook harmoniously combined with maximum cultural development."[9] The idea is a deep learning and invaluable education that requires engaging in things that matter in the world. As a black preacher, I have also learned hermeneutical humility by understanding how to distinguish the biblical interpretation from other cultural understandings.

Dr. Cornel West holds the prestigious Dietrich Bonhoeffer Chair at Union Theological Seminary. He is a renowned professor, teaching courses on the works of Dietrich Bonhoeffer, philosophy of religion, African American critical thought, and a broad range of other subjects. His interests mainly focus on classic works, philosophy, politics, cultural theory, literature, and music. Dr. West previously held the professor of public philosophy position at Harvard University and is currently a professor emeritus at Princeton University. In his essay "The Moral Obligations of Living in a Democratic Society," he said, "Empathy is not simply a matter of trying to imagine what others are going through but having the will to muster enough courage to do something about it. In a way, empathy is predicated upon hope."[10]

Along this line, I remember vividly when a preacher suddenly shifted from spiritual matters to the pressing social issues of the day. They would speak of police brutality, the inequity in the education system, the drug epidemic, the struggles for jobs, and the importance of black unity. To me, it seemed like these preachers had an uncanny ability to weave biblical stories with the contemporary struggles of black America. David facing Goliath mirrored our fight against systemic racism; Moses leading the Israelites out of Egypt symbolized our ongoing march toward true equality.

Nevertheless, it was not just their words that impacted me—it was their actions. Many of these preachers were on the front lines of protests, leading marches, advocating for policy changes, and providing platforms for young activists. They were living

9. *Merriam-Webster*, s.v. "paideia," https://www.merriam-webster.com/dictionary/paideia.

10. GreatHearts Institute, "Cornell West."

embodiments of the belief that faith without works is dead. These actions deeply inspired me. The preachers in my community demonstrated that it was possible to be both spiritually and socially conscious, that one could pray on Sunday and protest on Monday. Standing up against social injustices was a civic duty and a divine one. These early exposures planted seeds in me that grew into a profound appreciation for the interconnectedness of spirituality and activism. I learned that fighting for justice was not about being against others but about being for our community.

Years later, I reflect on those formative experiences and the invaluable lessons those black preachers imparted. Black preachers have the power of voice and should use it to stand up for what is right. They instilled in me a sense of responsibility to be a change agent. They showed that we, too, could be agents of change and champions for justice. Even today, as I continue to see and challenge racial injustice, poverty, white supremacy, and socioeconomic disparities, I can continue the long-lasting legacy of black pastors and preachers who helped shape and inspire me to believe in the power of faith united with action.

This book was written to recognize the importance of the African American missional pastors who have effected social change through the power of preaching, primarily in Florida. My argument is that with the leadership of black missional pastors in Florida, the African American people have achieved some equity and equality in education, housing, public policy, and the marketplace. As part of this evaluation of the effectiveness of black preaching, this researcher will survey two different social justice preachers of the Lord's church in Florida.

SIGNIFICANCE OF THIS PROJECT: DEFINING THE ISSUE

This book addresses the need for written history and scholarship on African American preaching in America, particularly in Florida. It highlights the many contributions that African American homiletics and homileticians have made in the fight for equity and equality through "social justice preaching." Colleen Murphy, in a medically reviewed article on Health, defines equity and equality. "Although 'equity' and 'equality' are often used interchangeably, they are different. Equity is the distribution of resources based on need, while equality is the even distribution of resources to all people, regardless of need."[11] Murphy said that equality and equity should be considered separate. While both concepts involve fairness and justice, how society achieves them and what they ultimately look like are different. According to Murphy, equity must be achieved first in order to have equality. "Equality assumes that everybody is the same and everybody needs the same thing."[12] However, "some people need more because they started with less," according to the United Nations.[13]

Historically, the topic of social justice in preaching has been challenging to define and has, at times, been too broadly defined. In this discussion, social justice preaching emphasizes believers' moral responsibility to engage with and rectify societal injustices within American society, viewing the issue through biblical themes. Social justice preaching encourages collective action through community service, activism, nonviolent protest, and other communal efforts to bring about societal change. For this reason, social justice preaching is controversial. Dr. Hyveth Williams, DMin, is the doctor of ministry program director and professor of homiletics at the Seventh-day Adventist Theological Seminary, Andrews University, Berrien Springs, Michigan. She writes, "Therefore, preaching social justice has become a polarizing proposition for many preachers because people seem to readily conclude the sermon will focus on inconvenient truths, primarily about systemic racism."[14]

The South African Anglican Bishop Desmond Tutu once said, "If you are neutral in injustice, you have chosen the side of the oppressor. If an elephant has its foot on the tail of a mouse

11. Murphy, "What's the Difference."
12. Murphy, "What's the Difference."
13. Murphy, "What's the Difference."
14. Williams, "Preaching Social Justice," 19.

and you say that you are neutral, the mouse will not appreciate your neutrality."[15] His words encapsulate a powerful moral stance that has reverberated through history. This statement challenges missional pastors and leaders to reflect on their role in addressing injustices and underscores the ethical imperative of taking a stand. At the heart of Tutu's statement lies a moral philosophy that rejects moral passivity and calls for active engagement in the face of injustice. Pastors and leaders inadvertently contribute to perpetuating injustice and inequality by choosing not to take a stand. Moreover, neutrality can signal a lack of empathy or concern for the marginalized and oppressed. In today's interconnected world, issues of injustice are pervasive and multifaceted, ranging from systemic racism and discrimination to economic inequality. Tutu's words serve as a call to action, urging missional pastors and leaders to take a stand and be agents of positive change in their communities.

Helmut Richard Niebuhr, better known as H. Richard Niebuhr, was one of the leading theologians of the twentieth century who wrote a fascinating book many years ago titled *Christ and Culture*. In this book, he gives us several metaphors that I have always retained in my consciousness of how Christians have historically approached faith in the context of culture. He begins his book by defining both Christ and culture. Niebuhr explains that Christ "is a great teacher and lawgiver who in what he said of God and the moral law so persuades the mind and will that there is henceforth no escape for him."[16] Niebuhr also defines culture as the "artificial, secondary environment" which man superimposes on the natural. "It comprises language, habits, ideas, beliefs, customs, social organization, inherited artifacts, technical processes, and values."[17] "Culture, secondly, is human achievement. We distinguish it from nature by noting the evidences of human purposiveness of effort."[18]

Next, he lists three critical choices of various ways in which Christians can live in our culture and social existence, based on

15. Ratcliffe, "Desmond Tutu."

16. Niebuhr, *Christ and Culture*, 12.

17. Niebuhr, *Christ and Culture*, 32.

18. Niebuhr, *Christ and Culture*, 33.

the way Christ interacted with culture. First, he says that "Christ is above the culture."[19] Because he is above the culture, you and I who follow him are expected to lift men and women, boys and girls, up to him. Our aspirations should be in line with Christ in terms of what he demands of us. Then he said, "Christ is in the culture."[20] He is not absent from the experiences that we have from day to day, that he is the Word made flesh. He is the Incarnate One who dwells among us, identifies with our issues, participates in our drama, and leads us into reconciliation. However, Niebuhr says there is a third context in which we must understand Jesus Christ. He is not only above the culture, he is not only in the culture, but there are times when he is "against the culture."[21]

If ever there was a time that Jesus Christ had a message that rails against American culture, I think that day is now. It is almost as if we can hear the writer of Judges writing, in that long-ago day of Old Testament antiquity, a word prevalent for our time—namely, we are sitting each one of us beneath our vine and fig tree, doing as we please. Theologians call this age a *postmodern age*, an age in which there are no absolutes. In an age in which everything is relative, we do as we please with no sense at all about the welfare and well-being of other people. It is a "do-your-own-thing" generation. Not only is it damnable, but it is destructive, and if we are not careful, Western civilization as we know it will perish from around us.

Why is it that the church seems to be quiet, muted, and silent when so many issues are pressing upon us? There is the issue of materialism on the one hand; there is the issue of heathenism on another. There are the issues of immorality, racism, classism, and sexism. If you will, all of these giants and titans are alive and doing well. Many of us live comfortable and convenient lives, and because we are living comfortable and convenient lives, these giants seek to destroy us.

Barbara Brown Taylor, a best-selling author, teacher, and Episcopal priest, said, "The only clear line I draw these days is this:

19. Niebuhr, *Christ and Culture*, 116 (ch. 4, "Christ Above Culture").

20. Niebuhr, *Christ and Culture*, 83 (ch. 3, "The Christ of Culture").

21. Niebuhr, *Christ and Culture*, 45 (ch. 2, "Christ Against Culture").

when my religion tries to come between me and my neighbor, I will choose my neighbor. . . . Jesus never commanded me to love my religion."[22] That is one main issue today with mainstream black pastors, such as Dr. Tony Evans, Voddie Baucham, and Bishop T. D. Jakes, that I have observed. In reflecting and pondering on their silence, is it possible that perhaps, if tithes come from white donors, some preachers choose their religious white evangelical base, which financially supports and undergirds their ministry platforms, over black people and the issues of racism and inequality? There may be a fine line between catering to your base and not addressing real issues from the pulpit. They stand to risk losing their financial support by lending their powerful voices and influences on social justice issues.

It seems apparent that one must be very careful and choose wisely what issues one will address from the pulpit in this day and age to avoid getting canceled. The "cancel culture" is very powerful. "[Cancel culture is] destroying a person's career or reputation based on past events in which that person participated or past statements that person has made, even if their beliefs or opinions have changed."[23] Cancel culture is "the practice or tendency of engaging in mass canceling as a way of expressing disapproval and exerting social pressure."[24]

The perspective of Voddie Baucham is important to this topic. Baucham serves as dean of the School of Divinity at African Christian University in Lusaka, Zambia, and is also a pastor and church planter. Baucham does not approve of social justice critical race theory (CRT). In 1848, Karl Marx and Friedrich Engels opened the Communist Manifesto by stating, "A specter is haunting Europe—the specter of Communism."[25] Baucham believes critical theory is founded in Marxist ideology, not biblical justice. "Critical Theory and its subsets, Critical Race Theory-Intersectionality (CRT-I) and

22. Taylor, *Holy Envy*, 208.

23. Vogels et al., "Americans and 'Cancel Culture.'"

24. *Merriam-Webster*, s.v. "cancel culture," https://www.merriam-webster.com/dictionary/cancel%20culture.

25. Marx and Engels, *Communist Manifesto*, 1.

Critical Social Justice (C.S.J.) can be traced through the Frankfurt School and Antonio Gramsci back to Marx's Conflict Theory."[26] Baucham and those who believe like him are opposed to CRT, which examines the laws that govern the United States and systemic racism. Baucham stated, "I have pursued justice my entire Christian life. Yet I am about as anti-social justice as they come—not because I have abandoned my obligation to 'strive for peace with everyone, and for the holiness without which no one will see the Lord' (Hebrews 12:14), but because I believe the current concept of social justice is incompatible with biblical Christianity."[27] Baucham provides several reasons to support his stance on the current cultural differences or, as he calls it, "fault lines" on race in America. Baucham quotes author and history professor at Simmons College of Kentucky in Louisville Jemar Tisby, PhD: "Opponents of racial justice often deploy labels such as Communism, Marxism, socialism, and critical race theory as attempts to set the limits of discourse and control the conversation. It's not new, but it is a resilient tactic that has deceived too many."[28] Ultimately, there are those on both sides of the fault line. "Those" refers not to oppressors existing equally on both sides, but to groups holding opposing interpretive positions on social justice and race in America. On one side are individuals—often associated with positions of historical and structural power—who either benefit from, deny, minimize, or fail to recognize systemic racism, privilege, and gender hierarchy. On the other side are individuals and communities—particularly women and black and brown people—who experience marginalization and oppression and therefore interpret social justice through the lens of lived inequality and systemic injustice. These opposing groups differ fundamentally in how they define justice, power, and responsibility within American society,

26. Baucham, *Fault Lines*, xii–xiii.

27. Baucham, *Fault Lines*, 5.

28. Jemar Tisby (@jemartisby), "Opponents of racial justice often deploy labels," Twitter, Aug. 28, 2020, 12:09 p.m., https://x.com/JemarTisby/status/1299378580510650370, cited in Baucham, *Fault Lines*, 225.

as Baucham describes the present "fault lines" in the cultural and theological debate.

In contrast to Baucham's stance, other scholars have examined the factors that shape the content and style of African American preaching on social justice issues. For example, the Reverend Kelly Brown Douglas argues that the black church's history of advocating for social justice has shaped its preaching style and content, particularly concerning issues such as violence, police brutality, white exceptionalism, and mass incarceration through the prison industrial complex. Douglas, a black Episcopal priest, dean of the Episcopal Divinity School at Union Theological Seminary, and professor of theology at Union New York, says, "The black church has a role to play, and it always has. It's been that institution that has been a resource of survival as well as resistance and liberation struggles for the black community."[29]

In contrast to Douglas and her zeal for the role of the black church, many pastors have forsaken their moral responsibilities, and the consequences of their actions—or inactions—in the face of injustice have empowered the oppressor.

SOCIAL JUSTICE BIBLICALLY DEFINED

Williams also writes about biblical social justice, which she defines thus: "Biblical Social Justice may therefore be defined as a divine mandate of faith and fundamental expression of Christian discipleship 'to make a right' one's relationship with God, others, and natural creation."[30] Many other theologians are making the connection between the Bible and justice. Timothy Keller, an American Calvinist pastor, preacher, theologian, and Christian apologist, writes in his book *Generous Justice: How God's Grace Makes Us Just*, "I have observed over the decades that when people see the

29. Banks, "From Ferguson to Baltimore."

30. Williams "Preaching Social Justice," 20.

beauty of God's grace in Christ, it leads them powerfully toward justice."[31]

Keller introduces the reader to Mark R. Gornik, PhD, an author and the director of City Seminary of New York. Keller explains Mark Gornik's influence on the Croatian theologian Miroslav Volf. Volf explains his thoughts on American Christianity: "They deem it generally useless or at least unhelpful when it comes to healing even lesser social pathologies than the cycle of poverty, violence, and hopelessness."[32] He gets the epiphany from Gornik: "How could the dead streets receive life from a [seemingly] dead doctrine?"[33] I take this to mean that the urban setting, the city, or the streets are spiritually, socially, and morally barren or lifeless and need the impact of an active faith.

This dead doctrine of American Christianity aforementioned in this particular setting could be viewed as outdated, irrelevant, or ineffective. It begs the question: Can these ancient religious truths still bring hope and change to present-day challenges within the twenty-first century? The answer is *yes*; there is still healing and hope in the gospel of Jesus Christ. This doctrine will come alive once this grace is proudly preached and practiced. Keller's book is a resource that will help missional pastors become change agents in their respective communities.

Mark Gornik's research about segregation and poverty in Sandtown reminds us of how this idea of what Volf saw in Gornik's ministry in New York connects with my concerns about the pastor's preaching about social justice in Florida. Keller "makes a compelling case that 'systematic exclusion' creates many poor inner-city neighborhoods."[34] Gornik also observes the economic realities of Sandtown residents; their poverty "was not initially the product of individual irresponsible behavior or family breakdown. . . . A complex range of structural factors led to the exclusion of

31. Keller, *Generous Justice*, xx.

32. Volf, "Shopkeeper's Gold," 138, cited in Keller, *Generous Justice*, 105.

33. Volf, "Shopkeeper's Gold," 138, cited in Keller, *Generous Justice*, 105; brackets original.

34. Keller, *Generous Justice*, 35.

the neighborhood's residents from the resources they needed to thrive."[35] The decline of manufacturing jobs and an increase in service sector jobs often led to lower wages for blacks, and some white companies refused even to hire blacks. This led to a decline in property value and deteriorating housing conditions.

Gornik's work stressed the resilience and activism of the African American Sandtown residents. Local pastors led the community members in grassroots organizing and church-led initiatives that improved their neighborhood. The neighborhood had been impacted by destructive policies. "For example, intrusive freeways were built to enable people to live in the suburbs and commute by car to center city jobs, and many of these building programs bisected or devasted urban neighborhoods."[36] Also, "Gornik's research and narrative make a convincing case—the poverty of an inner-city neighborhood like Sandtown was not initially the product of individual irresponsible behavior of family breakdown."[37]

Timothy Keller's observations about African American theology and social justice are vital. Keller came to see himself as a racist through his African American friend Elward Ellis. His friend made an excellent point which led Keller to reflect and write, "We made our cultural biases into moral principles and then judged people of other races as being inferior."[38] What a powerful statement. Every culture has values, practices, and norms that help guide and shape their behaviors. These cultural biases form the foundation for one's perspective on the world and influence how individuals perceive other cultures within the society.

This is what is known as ethnocentrism. Ethnocentrism is "the attitude that one's own group, ethnicity, or nationality is superior to others."[39] Universalizing one's cultural standards and values instead of recognizing that these standards and values are

35. Keller, *Generous Justice*, 35.

36. Keller, *Generous Justice*, 37.

37. Keller, *Generous Justice*, 37.

38. Keller, *Generous Justice*, xvii.

39. *Merriam-Webster*, s.v. "ethnocentrism," https://www.merriam-webster.com/dictionary/ethnocentrism.

relative to one's culture is a problem. When we elevate our cultural practices, "the way we do things" becomes "the way things should be done." Ethnocentric people judge other cultures based on the standards of their own culture. Moreover, that is very easy to do. We must try to see things from others' points of view.

When we extend grace to others, the love of God is demonstrated. The importance of a socially engaged missional pastor cannot be overstated in today's complex, global, and interconnected world. A socially engaged missional pastor actively contributes to the broader social and political conversation while fulfilling their traditional pastoral roles within their church and community. Socially engaged missional pastors serve as a moral compass for their congregation by providing guidance and perspective on pressing social issues and concerns within the community. They empower their communities to overcome economic, social, spiritual, and political challenges. Socially engaged pastors advocate for the rights and well-being of marginalized and oppressed people. Missional pastors must use their platform to address social issues such as poverty, racial injustice, sexism, and discrimination by amplifying the voices of those who are often overlooked.

Father Dan Groody, PhD, is also concerned with a biblical definition of social justice that describes concern for low-income people. Groody, an author and associate professor of theology and global affairs, is the vice president and associate provost for undergraduate education at the University of Notre Dame in Notre Dame, Indiana. According to Groody, "the Narrative of the Poor takes shape most often around those who are victims of society's greed, exploitation, and manipulation, that is, those who suffer the consequences of empire."[40] The Hebrews in the Bible are referred to as the poor and oppressed, as are the African Americans today. Groody also writes, "Some scholars believe that the term 'Hebrew' itself (*Apiru*, *Habiru*) referred originally to a social class of poor and marginalized people in Canaan, and much of the Old Testament is about their story."[41]

40. Groody, *Globalization*, loc. 101.

41. Groody, *Globalization*, loc. 101.

James H. Cone, author, theologian, and father of black theology and black liberation theology, writes, "Since the biblical God stands against the culture of the oppressors, must we assume that God is the God of the culture of the oppressed?"[42] Standing for biblical justice, Cone also states, "The consistent theme in Israelite prophecy is Yahweh's concern for the lack of social, economic, and political justice for those who are poor and unwanted in society."[43]

Willie J. Jennings, a Baptist minister from North Carolina who is an author and associate professor of systematic theology and Africana studies at Yale Divinity School in New Haven, Connecticut, writes, "I argue here that Christianity in the Western world lives and moves within a diseased social imagination."[44] Jennings believes that Christians in the West live from social imaginations that are sick, anemic, and lack a full theological perspective of modern society, one that counters racialization with Christian belonging. Jennings further postulates, "Christian theology now operates inside this diseased social imagination without the ability to discern how its intellectual and pedagogical performances reflect and fuel the problem, further crippling the communities it serves."[45] Jennings suggests that there is a gap between the church and the classroom, thus tainting the imagination of Christian intellectuals.

Jennings is also well aware of the racial tension that was all around. Like Jennings, I was made aware of the racial tension that was all around me. I even saw hate where the Bible said there should be love and division where there should have been unity. Jennings saw something seriously wrong from a Christian standpoint, which gave him a different hermeneutic or interpretive lens and enabled him to promote the way forward to a true Christian imagination. Jennings drives the point home that Christianity was meant to join both Jews and gentiles and, hence, blacks and whites today. Jennings said, "The most common way to narrate this

42. Cone, *God of the Oppressed*, 88.

43. Cone, *Black Theology of Liberation*, loc. 398.

44. Jennings, *Christian Imagination*, 6.

45. Jennings, *Christian Imagination*, 7.

historical reality of Western Christianity displayed in my backyard is to speak of different Christianities, white and black, or different culture expressions of Christianity, (European) immigrant and (African) slave, or even of sinful division by faith formed from the historical realities of slavery."[46] Jennings brings to the forefront his worldview, shaped chiefly by his mother and the Christian contradictions to Christian truth he witnessed as a child. Those contradictions dealt with matters of culture, race, and religion.

This is not just a historical or theological concern—it is a present reality. Take, for example, Florida Governor Ron DeSantis. DeSantis has led an aggressive campaign to erase, marginalize, and sanitize black history from public education in Florida. Under the banner of "anti-woke" policies, he signed legislation like the "Stop W.O.K.E. Act," which restricts how race-related topics can be taught in schools and workplaces. His administration has rejected advanced placement (AP) African American studies courses, arguing they lack educational value, and has downplayed slavery by promoting curriculum standards that suggest enslaved people benefited from slavery.[47] DeSantis presents himself as a defender of parental rights and traditional American values, but in reality, he is systematically undermining the truth about America's racial past and silencing the voices of black scholars, educators, and students. This is not just political posturing; it is a form of cultural and educational violence.

The Old Testament prophets were concerned with social justice. Micah 6:8 is an excellent example of biblical social justice preaching: "He has told you, O man, what is good; and what does the Lord require of you but to do justice, and to love kindness, and to walk humbly with your God?" (ESV). Therefore, we should think deeply about the subject. What does the Lord require of us? The prophet lists three things: to do justice, to love kindness, and to walk humbly with your God. The Lord says, "I want you to do justice for all. Give everyone their due—friend or foe, rich or poor, whatever the culture or color. Do justice!" Remembering how God

46. Jennings, *Christian Imagination*, 4.

47. Contorno, "African American Studies Course."

dealt with the nation of Israel in the Old Testament helps to shape our social responsibility and social justice today as church-based social activists.

LITERATURE REVIEW AND METHODOLOGY

This book evaluates the theological considerations drawn from a literature review of research published in recent years about African American preaching and social justice. It involves engaging mainly the following two themes: religious/civil persecution of African Americans in the South, particularly in Florida, during slavery; and the Civil Rights Movement and the preaching that sustained it. A distinction was made between those literary sources that are primary and those that are secondary. Also, sources included information from secular and Christian documentaries, reviews, books, journals, autobiographies, and congressional hearings. Examining social justice and preaching also involved qualitative research, specifically ethnographic interviews. Therefore, other interlocutors were the case studies drawn from the interviewees who participated in the research. The interviews explored how certain pastors approach social justice issues in their preaching, the factors that shaped their thinking about social justice, and their content and style. For example, an interviewee with firsthand knowledge of events during the Civil Rights Movement, Deacon Pete Boyd, contributed to the study.

Research Questions

Some of the questions posed to guide the gathering of historical data are featured below:

1. What impact did preachers have before the Civil Rights Movement?
2. How have African American preachers influenced social movements like the Civil Rights Movement? How has preaching influenced the passing of legislation on social justice?

Some of the questions dealing with preaching in Florida are featured below:

3. How did Father Pinder and Reverend Steele make an impact in Florida through their preaching?
4. Are social justice issues important to African American preachers in Florida today? Why or why not?
5. However, is the risk of preaching on social justice issues perceived too great in our contemporary context?

DEFINITION OF TERMS

This book traces the development process in preaching according to a theory termed *constructivism*, whereby knowledge is acquired through reflection on experience. Also, since black preachers draw from lived experience for constructing their sermons, this discussion rests on aspects of *critical theory*. Critical theory is reflected in the idea that lived experience fuels preachers to critique one version of truth by bringing other truths to light. For example, Emmett Till's death inspired a movement and galvanized black Americans to seek legislation for equal rights. "One hundred days after Till's murder, Rosa Parks refused to give up her seat to a white passenger on a Montgomery city bus and was arrested for violating Alabama's bus segregation laws. Reverend Jesse Jackson told Vanity Fair (1988), 'Rosa said she thought about going to the back of the bus. But then she thought about Emmett Till, and she couldn't do it.'"[48]

The following terms are defined to help the reader understand how they are used in this study:

Qualitative research "is multi-method in focus, involving an interpretive, naturalistic approach to its subject matter. This means that qualitative researchers study things in their natural settings,

48. Smithsonian, "Emmett Till's Death."

attempting to make sense of, or interpret, phenomena in terms of the meanings people bring to them."[49]

Ethnography is "the study and systematic recording of human cultures: a descriptive work produced from such research."[50] It is a core method in cultural anthropology and sociology that seeks to understand the lived experiences, values, and practices of a group of people from their own perspective. Central to ethnographic research is the use of in-depth interviews, participant observation, and narrative inquiry to collect detailed data about social life. As stated above, interviews are considered a primary method in ethnography and will be used to capture the personal experiences of black preachers. These interviews not only allow for the gathering of firsthand testimonies but also provide rich, contextual insights into the dynamics of race, faith, and justice in Florida. As Swinton and Mowat point out, "a key tool of qualitative research that is obviously deeply linked to the researcher is the interview or, more precisely, the in-depth interview."[51] This paper's in-depth interviews provide evidence of social change in Florida through eyewitness accounts. Swinton and Mowat further affirm that "interviews are concentrated human encounters that take place between the researcher who is seeking knowledge and the research participant who is willing to share their experience and knowledge."[52] In this study, the in-depth interview functions as both a method of documentation and a source of prophetic insight, offering evidence of transformation through narrative.

Constructivism "is a learning theory which holds that knowledge is best gained through a process of reflection and active construction in the mind. Thus, knowledge is an intersubjective interpretation. The learner must consider the information being

49. Swinton and Mowat, *Practical Theology*, loc. 40.

50. *Merriam-Webster*, s.v. "ethnography," https://www.merriam-webster.com/dictionary/ethnography.

51. Swinton and Mowat, *Practical Theology*, loc. 71.

52. Swinton and Mowat, *Practical Theology*, loc. 71.

taught and—based on past experiences, personal views, and cultural background—construct an interpretation."[53]

Critical theory asserts that "reality may be objective but truth is continually contested by competing groups."[54] Neil Shenvi and Pat Sawyer, in their book *Critical Dilemma*, write,

> Critical theory began in the early 1920s with the Frankfurt School, a school of social theory and critical philosophy first affiliated with the Institute for Social Research at Goethe University in Frankfurt, Germany. *Critical Theory* often refers to the Frankfurt school and its direct descendants when capitalized. However, critical social theory (which is sometimes referred to as "critical theory"—note the lower case letters) is an umbrella category that encompasses the numerous critical social theories (or critical theories) that have been spawned by and have developed within the critical tradition: feminist theory, postcolonialism, critical pedagogy, queer theory, and critical race theory, among others.[55]

Lived experience encompasses "the things that someone has experienced themselves, especially when these give the person a knowledge or understanding that people who have only heard about such experiences do not have."[56]

Hegemony is "leadership or dominance, especially by one country or social group over others."[57]

Equity is "the situation in which everyone is treated fairly according to their needs, and no group of people is given special treatment: a society based on equity and social justice."[58]

53. Huff, "Constructivism." See also Mascolo and Fischer, "Constructivist Theories."

54. Swinton and Mowat, *Practical Theology*, loc. 1282.

55. Shenvi and Sawyer, *Critical Dilemma*, 16.

56. *Cambridge Dictionary*, s.v. "lived experience," https://dictionary.cambridge.org/us/dictionary/english/lived-experience.

57. *Oxford Dictionary*, s.v. "hegemony," https://www.oed.com/search/advanced/Meanings?textTermTexto=hegemony&textTermOpto=Definition.

58. *Cambridge Dictionary*, s.v. "equity," https://dictionary.cambridge.org/us/dictionary/english/equity.

Equality is "the right of different groups of people to have a similar social position and receive the same treatment."[59]

Existential exegesis is "the close observation of life, which yields a rich storehouse of interesting, true stories illustrative of biblical precepts with which the hearer may identify."[60]

Embodied is "expressed, personified, or exemplified in concrete form."[61]

LIMITATIONS OF THE STUDY

This study contains certain limitations, some of which are inherent to the nature of qualitative and historical studies, and others that were intentionally imposed to limit the scope of the study. The researcher recognizes the following limitations and has attempted to account for their impact on the quality of the research. The primary limitation of this study is the researcher's subjectivity, but I have done my best to assess information objectively. However, I must also acknowledge that my interpretation has been shaped by a personal journey of constructivism—an ongoing process of piecing together knowledge informed not just by theory and scholarship but also by lived experience. I was born in Gary, Indiana, a city shaped by the legacy of the Great Migration. My grandparents and parents moved there from the South in search of opportunity and dignity. What they found, however, was a world that demeaned their humanity. They were called names like *boy*, *uncle*, and worse—epithets that echoed the same rhetoric used to shame the peaceful protesters of the Civil Rights Movement. They were forced to step off sidewalks to make way for white pedestrians, to drink from separate fountains, to enter through back doors. Every institution—from hospitals to courtrooms, from legislation to law enforcement—reminded them they were seen as less than.

59. *Cambridge Dictionary*, s.v. "equality," https://dictionary.cambridge.org/us/dictionary/english/equality.

60. Simmons and Thomas, *Preaching with Sacred Fire*, 7–8.

61. Dictionary.com, s.v. "embodied," https://www.dictionary.com/browse/embodied.

These painful yet formative realities are not just part of my family history; they are part of my epistemology. They inform how I see the world, approach this research, and understand the significance of giving voice to the marginalized. The second limitation of this study is the lack of written history of African American preaching within the black ecclesiastical community. Third, there is not much written historical background on the role and preaching of women within the black church, particularly in the South. Last, I have intentionally limited my focus to examining social justice preaching in Florida.

CHAPTER TWO

THE CONTEXT OF THE AFRICAN AMERICAN PREACHER

THIS CHAPTER WILL DESCRIBE the broad landscape in which the need for social justice in the United States is situated. Edward Franklin Frazier, PhD, affectionately known as E. Franklin Frazier, was an author, distinguished professor, and American socialist; he writes, "The Negro slave found in Christianity a theology and a new orientation towards the world at large, and in doing so, he adapted the Christian religion to his psychological and social needs."[1] Therefore, the material will cover America's historical problem of race relations, spanning from slavery and Reconstruction to the civil rights era and postmodern society. Frazier also captures the words of an ex-slave about the pioneer black preacher:

> Our preachers were usually plantation folks, just like the rest of us. Some man with a little education and who had been taught something about the Bible would be our preacher. The coloured folks had their code of religion, not nearly so complicated as the white man's religion, but more closely observed. . . . When we had our meetings of this kind, we held them in our own way and were not interfered with by the white folks.[2]

1. Frazier, *Negro Church in America*, 12.
2. Frazier, *Negro Church in America*, 16.

Furthermore, the chapter will highlight the significant historical events that formed and shaped African American social justice preaching throughout America and in Florida, including the establishment of the first African American churches, the emergence of black denominations, and the role of preaching during the Civil Rights Movement.

Henry H. Mitchell's book *Black Church Beginnings: The Long-Hidden Realities of the First Years* offers an insightful portrayal of the African American struggle to create religious societies and churches during the tough times of the transatlantic slave trade in the newly formed American colonies. The book, written by a leading expert on African American religion, gives an overview of the black church's birth, maturity, and matriculation from the eighteenth to the nineteenth centuries.

As depicted by Mitchell, the first African American churches faced immense hardships and obstacles, yet they persevered and thrived through faith and determination. Churches did not just organize; the black church's beginnings are intertwined with the experiences of enslaved Africans, their religious practices, and the development of a unique Christian tradition within American society. Mitchell masterfully guides readers through the developmental process of forming independent congregations. Despite the efforts of slaveholders trying to control and restrict religious activities among the enslaved population, African Americans began to form their own religious gatherings and worship spaces.

He truthfully studies the task of finding the role of early black preachers. Both enslaved and free black preachers played a crucial role in spreading Christianity within the African American community. They often held secret meetings and led worship services distinctly African American in character, which E. Franklin Frazier called the "Invisible Institution." "It is no exaggeration to say that the 'invisible institution' of the Negro church took root among the enslaved blacks."[3] The establishment of black churches opened new doors in which to engage the white power structure and culture through religious expression.

3. Frazier, *Negro Church in America*, 16.

SLAVERY AND THE AFRICAN AMERICAN PREACHER

According to Frederick Douglass, the abolitionist orator and writer who escaped slavery, "the preacher was one of the slave notabilities."[4] To understand the context of the African American preacher, one must delve into the historical backdrop of African Americans in the United States.

> In late August 1619, 20–30 enslaved Africans landed at Point Comfort, today's Fort Monroe in Hampton, Va., aboard the English privateer ship White Lion. In Virginia, these Africans were traded in exchange for supplies. Several days later, a second ship (Treasurer) arrived in Virginia with additional enslaved Africans.[5]

These are the first recorded enslaved Africans to arrive in England's mainland American colonies, which would later become the United States of America.

> The enslaved Africans brought to Virginia in 1619 were probably from the Kingdom of Ndongo in West Central Africa. They were Kimbundu-speaking people who shared a common cultural identity and brought advanced agricultural and industrial knowledge. Between 1618 and 1620, Portuguese colonizers allied with local Imbangala mercenaries to conquer Ndongo and enslave thousands of the kingdom's inhabitants.[6]

The African American experience is marked by centuries of slavery, lynching, Jim Crow segregation, racial oppression, and discrimination. Robin Blackburn, author and British historian, writes, "The acquisition of some twelve million captives on the coast of Africa between 1500 and 1870 helped to make possible the construction of one of the largest systems of slavery in human history."[7] The transatlantic slave trade was perhaps the most

4. Douglass, *Life and Times*, 31.
5. Hampton History Museum, "1619 Landing."
6. Austin, *1619*, 3.
7. Blackburn, *Making of New World*, 3.

significant global economic commodity from the sixteenth to the nineteenth Century. "Slave-grown tobacco, sugar, and cotton facilitated the birth of an expansive new world of consumption—one that was antithetical to slave rations and self-provision."[8] Many of the African slaves taken were Muslims and could be easily distinguished from the other groups of slaves. "Slaves who survived the Middle Passage encountered in their host society a violent hostility toward their culture and faith."[9] Although Africans had known slavery before, the transatlantic chattel slavery was different because of its racial prejudices. According to Dawn-Marie Gibson, PhD, professor of US history and African American Islam at Royal Holloway, University of London, "Many Muslim slaves arrived in the United States already literate and such were able to both write copies of the Qur'an from memory and pen autobiographies. . . . The most well-known of such autobiographies are Job Ben Solomon's and Ibrahim ar-Rahman's."[10] Gibson further postulates that "literacy clearly set Muslim slaves apart from their African counterparts."[11] The Muslim African slaves could be distinguished from other enslaved Africans by their literacy and adherence to Islam.

Looking back on this historic period, one must take an existential exegesis of the lives of those kidnapped from their country and sold to work in forced labor camps in a new country—their experiences, choices, and beliefs. Many of the African slaves became Christians, and even some of the Muslim slaves. This new slave religion, or black religion, gave the enslaved people power, and Christianity gave the slaves strength. From the crucible of slavery, three distinct forms of black religious life emerged in the American South.

First was what E. Franklin Frazier identified as the "invisible institution," a clandestine form of worship created by enslaved Africans who were denied the freedom to gather openly. As Frazier

8. Blackburn, *Making of New World*, 3.

9. Gibson, *History of the Nation of Islam*, 2.

10. Gibson, *History of the Nation of Islam*, 2.

11. Gibson, *History of the Nation of Islam*, 3.

explains, "It is no exaggeration to say that the 'invisible institution' of the Negro church took place among the enslaved blacks." [12] Albert J. Raboteau further clarifies that this invisible church was "the church of the slaves, hidden from the eyes of the master and nurtured in secret places such as the woods, brush arbors, and riverbanks."[13] Because discovery could result in punishment, enslaved people developed creative methods to conceal their worship. Raboteau notes that "in order to escape detection, slaves muffled the sound of their worship by placing pots over their mouths or hanging wet quilts around their meeting places."[14]

A second form of worship emerged in the praise house, which provided a limited and supervised space for religious expression. Raboteau observes that "praise houses were the most common institutional setting for slave worship where planters permitted religious meetings under supervision."[15] While these spaces allowed enslaved Africans to gather, they remained under white control. C. Eric Lincoln and Lawrence H. Mamiya describe the praise house as "a transitional form of Black religious expression—partially autonomous yet still subject to white surveillance and control."[16]

The third form consisted of white or biracial churches that allowed enslaved blacks to attend worship alongside whites, though always within rigid racial hierarchies. Donald G. Mathews explains that "slaves were admitted to white churches, but only on the condition that racial hierarchy be preserved in seating, leadership, and discipline."[17] Lincoln and Mamiya summarize this reality bluntly, stating, "In biracial churches, Blacks were members without power—present in worship but excluded from authority."[18]

In contrast, Northern churches permitted free blacks to worship but enforced segregation through gallery seating and spatial

12. Frazier, *Negro Church in America*, 23.

13. Raboteau, *Slave Religion*, 212.

14. Raboteau, *Slave Religion*, 213.

15. Raboteau, *Slave Religion*, 206.

16. Lincoln and Mamiya, *Black Church*, 9.

17. Mathews, *Religion in the Old South*, 150.

18. Lincoln and Mamiya, *Black Church*, 7.

marginalization. Richard Newman notes that "even in the North, free Blacks were commonly forced to sit in church galleries or along the walls, a practice that symbolized their marginal status within white Christianity."[19] James Cone adds that racial discrimination in Northern churches "differed only in degree, not in kind, from that of the South, as Blacks were segregated even in the house of God."[20]

Though the black church began as a hidden and constrained institution, it was never merely an imitation of white Christianity. Rather, as Raboteau emphasizes, "the slaves' religion was not merely an imitation of white Christianity but a creative adaptation shaped by resistance, suffering, and hope."[21] What began as an invisible institution ultimately evolved into one of the most powerful spiritual, social, and prophetic centers of African American life. The newly established black church believed in a God of love, justice, and vengeance. From the black church came the pioneer black preachers like David George, Reverend and Mr. Moses, Henry Evans, Black Harry, William Lott Carey, who did a lot of work in Liberia as a missionary, and Uncle Jack, a full-blooded African preacher who preached and won souls for Christ.

On March 4, 1861, Abraham Lincoln became the sixteenth president of the United States. Francis Bicknell Carpenter is best known for his painting *First Reading of the Emancipation Proclamation of President Lincoln* and his published memoir. President Lincoln called a cabinet meeting on September 22, 1862, to consider the issuing of his Emancipation Proclamation. Years before, he had made a promise to God. Louis A. Warren writes, "This statement was reported by Absalom Gentry, a son of Allen, who heard his father make the remark, and claimed that Abe said at this time, 'If I ever get a chance to hit this thing I'll hit it hard (slavery).' Related to Mrs. Bess V. Ehrmann and reported by her in a letter in the Lincoln National Life Foundation. The same remark is alleged to have been made by Abe on viewing the slave markets

19. Newman, *Freedom's Prophet*, 35.

20. Cone, *Spirituals and the Blues*, 31.

21. Raboteau, *Slave Religion*, 4.

on his second New Orleans trip."[22] President Lincoln commenced the cabinet meeting by saying,

> The time for the annunciation of the emancipation policy can be no longer delayed. Public sentiment will sustain it, many of my warmest friends and supporters demand it, and I have promised my God that I will do it. I made a solemn vow before God, that if General Lee was driven back to Pennsylvania, I would crown the result by the declaration of freedom to the slaves.[23]

He kept his promise on January 1, 1863. "Passed by Congress on January 31, 1865, and ratified on December 6, 1865, the 13th Amendment abolished slavery in the United States."[24] Molly Oshatz is a senior fellow and director of high school programs at the Zephyr Institute's Center for the Study of First Principles and a former assistant professor of history at San Francisco State University and Florida State University. According to Oshatz, "in order to account for its unique moral nature, antislavery moderates labeled slavery a social sin. Slavery, they explained, was a sin for which society, rather than the individual, might be responsible."[25]

Spiritual Leaders for the Reconstruction Era

The first African American preachers emerged during the era of slavery, often as spiritual leaders within enslaved populations. They played a crucial role in sustaining hope, resisting oppression, and passing down cultural traditions. Notable figures like Nat Turner, a preacher who led a slave rebellion "in the early hours of August 22, 1831,"[26] exemplified the historical significance of these religious leaders in advocating for freedom and justice. "Slaveholders used both psychological coercion and physical violence to prevent

22. Warren, *Lincoln's Youth*, 261.
23. Carpenter, *Six Months in the White House*, 89–90.
24. National Archives, "13th Amendment."
25. Oshatz, *Slavery and Sin*, 82.
26. Allyn, "Nat Turner's Rebellion."

slaves from disobeying their wishes. Often, the most efficient way to discipline slaves was to threaten to sell them."[27]

In order to endure the harsh conditions of slavery on cotton and sugar plantations, many slaves turned to religion. "The creation of family units, distant relations, and communal traditions allowed slaves to maintain religious beliefs, ancient ancestral traditions, and even names passed down from generation to generation in a way that challenged enslavement."[28] Here again, there must be an existential exegesis of the long-term psychological effects these harsh conditions had on the African slaves and their descendants.

Elizabeth Hobbs Keckley was formerly enslaved and became a successful seamstress, most notably known as Mary Todd Lincoln's personal modiste and confidante. Keckley writes, "Some of the freedmen and freedwomen had exaggerated ideas of liberty. To them, it was a beautiful vision, a land of sunshine, rest, and glorious promise."[29] In other words, most black people preferred assimilation over liberation. She adds,

> Often I heard them declare that they would rather go back to slavery in the South and be with their old masters than to enjoy the freedom of the North. I believe they were sincere in these declarations because dependence had become a part of their second nature, and independence brought with it the cares and vexations of poverty.[30]

For enslaved people, learning and scholarship were not permitted by the dominant culture in control of the African American community. The South is not known for its written history or scholarly preaching. For many years, black preaching, particularly in the South, was stereotyped as "folk preaching." Folk preaching was predominant in the period of preaching between 1750–1865. Folk preachers represented preachers without formal education and would include preachers like John Jasper, Sojourner Truth,

27. College Sidekick, "Life as a Slave."
28. College Sidekick, "Life as a Slave."
29. Keckley, *Behind the Scenes*, loc. 1186.
30. Keckley, *Behind the Scenes*, loc. 1186.

and Brother Copper. This was mostly an oral tradition in the form of narrative or storytelling. There is also a genre of preaching called "intellectual preaching." Intellectual or educated preaching is an academic approach practiced primarily by preachers attending college or seminary. Intellectual preaching was birthed in the North and used mainly by free blacks like John Chavis, Lemuel Haynes, and Absalom Jones.

Bishop Henry McNeal Turner (1834–1915) was a prominent African American preacher and advocate for civil rights and equality during the Reconstruction era in Georgia. He declared that Jesus was black and believed that we should reflect on our God as looking like us. Bishop Turner was on the level of Booker T. Washington and W. E. B. DuBois. Although he was born free in South Carolina, he constantly faced racial discrimination and violence throughout his life. Turner married Eliza Peacher in 1856, who was the daughter of a wealthy African American house builder, and to their union, fourteen children were born, four of whom survived into adulthood.

> Turner was born in 1834 in Newberry Courthouse, South Carolina, to Sarah Greer and Hardy Turner. Turner was never enslaved. His paternal grandmother was a white plantation owner. His maternal grandfather, David Greer, arrived in North America aboard a slave ship but, according to family legend, was found to have a tattoo with the Mandingo coat of arms, signifying his royal status. The South Carolinians decided not to sell Greer into slavery and sent him to live with a Quaker family.[31]

Turner was elected the twelfth bishop of the African Methodist Episcopal (AME) Church and fought against racial discrimination and inequality within the church and secular society. Turner advocated for the rights of African Americans to vote and hold political office. "In 1863, Turner was instrumental in organizing the First Regiment of U.S. Colored Troops in his own churchyard and was mustered into service as an army chaplain for that regiment."[32]

31. Angell, "Henry McNeal Turner."

32. Angell, "Henry McNeal Turner."

He was a key figure in helping to organize the AME Church with Richard Allen. "Turner was an extremely vigorous and successful bishop. In 1885 he became the first A.M.E. bishop to ordain a woman, Sarah Ann Hughes, to the office of deacon."[33]

It is clear that preaching has been the central worship- and community-building element in many black religious church traditions. Historically, black churches have provided spaces for empowerment and resistance against racial oppression. Women have played significant roles in some churches; however, very few have served as spiritual leaders despite facing discrimination and marginalization themselves.

Though not a preacher, Dr. Mary McLeod Bethune was a remarkable educator and civil rights activist who made significant contributions to American society during the early twentieth century. Her life story is a testament to her dedication to the advancement of African Americans through education, political activism, and community-building efforts. Bethune was born the daughter of formerly enslaved parents "on July 10, 1875, near Maysville, South Carolina; Bethune was one of the last of Samuel and Patsy McLeod's seventeen children. After the Civil War, her mother worked for her former owner until she could buy the land on which the family grew cotton. By age nine, Bethune could pick 250 pounds of cotton a day."[34]

THE AFRICAN AMERICAN CHURCH

African American missional pastors should demonstrate their care and concern by developing new missional churches and communities that seek fair and equal treatment for all people. The black church was birthed by enslaved people and formerly enslaved people who were oppressed and mostly illiterate. "The First African Baptist Church of Savannah, Georgia, began in 1773. This is said to be the oldest black church in North America. Originally

33. Angell, "Henry McNeal Turner."

34. Michals, "Mary McLeod Bethune."

called the First Colored Church, the pastoral life of George Liele's preaching is tied to its beginning."[35] The Reverend George Liele (1750–1828) was the "first African American to be ordained and first Baptist to go as a missionary to any other land (Jamaica)."[36]

Henry Mitchell argues that a deeper understanding of the roots and strengths of black preaching has led to significant correction in three areas of thought: "1) facts, truth, and the unbiased reporting of history; 2) improved black self-esteem, especially healthy spiritual self-esteem before God; and 3) marvelous improvement in communication skills, as African Traditional Religion's (A.T.R.'s) highly developed rhetoric and oratory have been accepted and effectively adapted into Christian worship."[37]

Throughout the years, several studies have dealt with the African American church, black theology, and religion in a standard way. The first among them is W. E. B. Dubois's book *The Negro Church*; followed by Carter G. Woodson's book *The History of the Negro Church*; and Benjamin E. Mays and Joseph W. Nicholson's book *The Negro's Church*. In his book *Somebody's Calling My Name: Black Sacred Music and Social Change*, the Reverend Dr. Wyatt Tee Walker Sr., author, pastor, civil rights leader, and activist, explores the profound influence of black sacred music, particularly spirituals and gospel music, on social change movements, including the Civil Rights Movement. According to Walker, "what Black people are singing religiously will provide a clue as to what is happening to them sociologically."[38]

A prime example of someone using preaching and singing to help advance the fight for equal rights was the Reverend C. L. Franklin. The Reverend C. L. Franklin, whose full name was Clarence LaVaughn Franklin, was a prominent Baptist preacher and civil rights activist. He was born on January 22, 1915, in Sunflower County, Mississippi, and passed away on July 27, 1984. "His preaching style was described as 'a perfect mixture of profound

35. African American Registry, "Black Church in America."

36. Neely, "Liele."

37. Mitchell, *Black Preaching*, loc. 30.

38. Walker, *Somebody's Calling My Name*, 17.

thought and emotional power,' and he became known nationwide as the man with the 'Million Dollar Voice.'"[39] Franklin was gifted as both a speaker and a singer.

He supported the efforts of leaders like Martin Luther King Jr. and participated in marches and protests to advance the cause of racial equality. Franklin's activism often made him a target of harassment and violence, but he remained steadfast in his commitment to justice and equality. Beyond his religious and political activities, Franklin was also the father of Aretha Franklin, the legendary "Queen of Soul." His influence on her musical career and her life was profound, as he encouraged her talent and supported her aspirations from a young age. During the height of his career, Franklin was the premiere black pastor in America.

Denominationalism

Following slavery, black Americans first established their dedicated places for worship and education, like churches and schools. According to Dictionary.com, *denominationalism* is "denominational or sectarian spirit or policy; the tendency to divide into denominations or sects."[40] These religious groups, sects, or traditions characteristically share a common religious heritage or beliefs but may differ in interpretation or church polity. "Historically, the Black Church in the United States has been composed of seven denominations: the African Methodist Episcopal Church; the African Methodist Episcopal Zion Church; the Christian Methodist Episcopal Church; the Church of God in Christ; and three National Baptist Conventions which convene Black Baptist congregations: the National Baptist Convention of America, the National Baptist Convention, USA, Inc., and the Progressive National Baptist Convention, Inc. Black denominations also include Southern Missionary Baptists and non-denominational churches."[41] Methodists

39. Detroit Historical Society, "Franklin."

40. Dictionary.com, s.v. "denominationalism," https://www.dictionary.com/browse/denominationalism.

41. FEMA, *Engagement Guidelines.*

and Baptists were the first two denominations to really connect with black Protestant Christians in America. Absalom Jones was a significant figure in African American and religious history. "Absalom Jones was America's first black priest. Born into slavery in Delaware at a time when slavery was being debated as immoral and undemocratic, he taught himself to read, using the New Testament as one of his resources."[42] Jones, possessing a prominent role as a religious leader, fervently championed the rights and dignity of African Americans. Moreover, he skillfully leveraged his influential position within the church to vociferously condemn the blights of slavery and racism while passionately promoting the causes of social justice and equality. "In 1784, Jones served as a lay minister for the black membership at St. George's Methodist Episcopal Church with his friend, Richard Allen, and together they established the Free African Society to aid in the emancipation of slaves and to offer sustenance and spiritual support to widows, orphans, and the poor."[43] His life and work paved the way for greater inclusion and representation of African Americans within the Episcopal Church.

Baptist and Methodist preachers went around preaching a gospel that the enslaved people could identify with. They were illiterate and were not able to read the Bible. The Baptist and Methodist preachers gave the enslaved people a sense of moral code, and the enslaved people heard the difference between right and wrong. The plantation was a social place in which whites and blacks worshiped together. House servants also attended family prayers. They worshiped on a segregated basis. Blacks preached under white supervisors. The vast majority of enslaved people sought meaning through Christianity. Some may call it escapism, but it gave them hope. They went toward a positive direction in God instead of a negative direction in their situation.

These churches became hubs for social and political activism, and African American preachers became prominent voices in the struggle for civil rights and equality. Religiously, African American preachers draw from a diverse theological heritage.

42. Archives of the Episcopal Church, "Reverend Absalom Jones."

43. Archives of the Episcopal Church, "Reverend Absalom Jones."

While many are part of predominantly black denominations like the AME Church, the National Baptist Association USA, or the Church of God in Christ (COGIC), others are part of multiracial congregations like the Assemblies of God. This diversity in religious affiliation reflects the broader American religious landscape.

Notable preachers included Richard Allen, a successful businessman. Bishop Allen, a Methodist, preached to his master and won his freedom. In 1816, Bishop Allen started the AME Church in a blacksmith's office and preached from the anvil in Philadelphia, Pennsylvania.

"The AMEC grew from the Free African Society," which had been founded in Philadelphia in 1787 by Richard Allen, Absalom Jones, and others. [44] After black worshipers were forcibly removed from prayer at St. George's Methodist Episcopal Church, Allen led a movement to establish the Bethel AME, securing its independence through successful court cases in 1807 and 1815.

In 1821, James Varick founded the African Methodist Episcopal Zion Church (AMEZ) in New York. In 1870, the Colored Methodist Episcopal (CME) Church, now the "Christian Methodist Episcopal Church . . . was founded in Jackson, Tennessee, by 41 former slaves."[45]

The Niagara Movement began in the 1900s. "The Niagara Movement was a movement of African American intellectuals founded in 1905 at Niagara Falls by such prominent men as W. E. B. DuBois and William Monroe Trotter. The movement was dedicated to obtaining civil rights for African Americans."[46] After Reconstruction, the Niagara Movement was formed in response to the racial discrimination and violence African Americans experienced in the United States.

> The Niagara Movement renounced Booker T. Washington's accommodation policies set forth in his famed "Atlanta Compromise" speech ten years earlier. The Niagara Movement's manifesto is, in the words of Du Bois, "We

44. African Methodist Episcopal, "Our History."
45. CME Church, "Christian Methodist Episcopal Church."
46. Electronic Oberlin Group, "Niagara Movement."

> want full manhood suffrage and we want it now. . . . We are men! We want to be treated as men. And we shall win." They invited 59 well known African American businessmen to a meeting that summer in western New York. On July 11 [through] 14, 1905, on the Canadian side of Niagara Falls, twenty-nine men met and formed a group they called the Niagara Movement. The name came because of the location and the "mighty current" of protest they wished to unleash.[47]

W. E. B. DuBois, the first black to attain a PhD from Harvard in the United States, was named the Niagara Movement leader during their secret inaugural meeting in the home of Mrs. Mary T. Talbert (who was a prominent member of black high society), and the newly elected leadership quickly split into various committees to lobby against Jim Crow and send circulars and protest letters to President Theodore Roosevelt. Even though the organization managed to establish a total of thirty branches and secure a handful of isolated civil rights triumphs at the local level, it grappled with inherent organizational fragility, financial constraints, and the absence of a fixed headquarters or dedicated staff, ultimately failing to garner widespread support from the masses. "In 1909, the Niagara Movement was hampered by a lack of funds."[48] Its legacy lived on through the continued struggle for racial equality and justice in the United States. In 1909–1910, the National Association for the Advancement of Colored People (NAACP) was established.

Within the broader history of American Christianity, the Baptist tradition did not originate in the black church; however, it became one of the most significant denominational expressions within the black church in the United States. As African Americans were excluded from white Baptist institutions, they formed their own autonomous bodies, giving rise to distinct black Baptist denominations. The National Baptist Convention, USA (NBC USA), the National Baptist Convention of America International

47. Circle Association, "Niagara Movement."

48. Electronic Oberlin Group, "Niagara Movement."

(NBCA), and the Progressive National Baptist Convention (PNBC) represent the three major denominational streams of the black Baptist church. One notable Baptist preacher who embodied this tradition's commitment to justice and equality was the Reverend Dr. Adam Clayton Powell Jr., a prominent African American pastor, politician, and civil rights activist. As "an effective leader and agent for change, Powell pushed boundaries in order to better the lives of African Americans, contributing to the early history of the civil rights movement."[49] Powell was born on November 29, 1908, in New Haven, Connecticut, but grew up in New York City. He graduated from Colgate University and Columbia University, where he earned a master's degree in religious education.

Powell became the pastor of the Abyssinian Baptist Church in Harlem, New York, in 1937, succeeding his father, Adam Clayton Powell Sr. He transformed the church into a center for political and social activism, advocating for civil rights, economic justice, and fair employment practices. In addition to his role as a pastor, Powell was a trailblazing politician. He served in the New York City Council from 1941 to 1945, becoming the first African American to represent Harlem.

Powell was elected to the United States House of Representatives, representing Harlem, until 1971. During his time in Congress, Powell fought tirelessly for civil rights and social justice. He challenged segregation and discrimination, pushed for anti-poverty legislation, and advocated for fair housing and education reforms. According to Stanford University's Martin Luther King Jr. Research and Education Institute,

> Powell and King traveled together to Ghana to celebrate that country's independence in 1957. When Powell was facing a difficult reelection the following year, King pledged his "wholehearted support," writing: "As I see it, the attacks upon you are in reality an effort to destroy the Negroes' political independence, and remove from the legislature an uncompromising voice."[50]

49. Jeffres and Sportelli, "Adam Clayton Powell Jr."

50. Stanford University, "Powell."

Powell was chosen chairman of the House Education and Labor Committee. "As chairman, Powell played a crucial role in moving Lyndon Johnson's progressive War on Poverty legislation through Congress."[51] Powell was a skilled orator and a master of parliamentary procedure, using his influence and charisma to advance the cause of civil rights. After leaving Congress, Powell remained active in public life until his death on April 4, 1972. Powell left a legacy of leadership and activism and should be remembered for his contributions to the Civil Rights Movement and his commitment to social justice preaching.

In his book *The Cost of Discipleship*, Dietrich Bonhoeffer, the German Protestant theologian, writes about his experience at a black Baptist church in New York in 1930. Adam Clayton Powell Sr. was the senior pastor, and Adam Clayton Powell Jr. was the assistant pastor. What strikes me most about Dietrich Bonhoeffer's story, as Eric Metaxas relays it in the foreword, is that he was determined to live according to his faith. I was also pleasantly surprised to learn that Bonhoeffer's life was changed not by his short time at Union Theological Seminary but by "what he experienced at an African American church in Harlem."[52] His experience that Sunday at the historic Abyssinian Baptist Church validated what he felt on the inside but had not found in Germany or among his (white) institutions. "Dietrich saw that they were not merely religious, but rather were the church, the people of God living out their faith with a joy Bonhoeffer had never seen."[53] That experience he received from visiting and worshiping with the black church in New York gave him the spark he needed to fulfill his destiny.

He returned to Germany filled with vigor and vitality and saw the afflictions of Jews and compared them with the injustices he had witnessed African Americans speaking out against. He coined the phrase "religionless Christianity" in his critique of religion, meaning Christian faith goes beyond religion and worship. "Bonhoeffer himself used the expression 'religionless Christianity' only

51. Stanford University, "Powell."

52. Metaxas, foreword to Bonhoeffer, *Cost of Discipleship*, 8.

53. Metaxas, foreword to Bonhoeffer, *Cost of Discipleship*, 8.

in the famous letter of April 30, 1944."[54] There must also be a call to action and a deep-seated conviction of will to right wrongs and to help the helpless.

The pages found in the section "Memoir" were written by Bonhoeffer's brother-in-law Gerhard Leibholz, a German legal scholar who passed away in 1982. Leibholz offers us a term he called *Christian humanism*. Humanism highlights man's moral responsibilities in life and applies them to emotions, happiness, and human progress, without due humility because it seeks to be and do without God. Christian humanism is contrary to humanism as it seeks to understand one's personal faith walk in the person of Jesus Christ. "Man must follow him who has served and passed through this world as the living, the dying, and risen Lord."[55] Bonhoeffer gave his life for Christian humanism. He followed his convictions, and most importantly, he followed his Savior. Bonhoeffer provides a permanent example of his theology: "When Christ calls a man, he bids him come and die."[56] I believe Bonhoeffer's connection with the Abyssinian Baptist Church was a divine connection that prepared and propelled him to action upon his return to Germany.

Pentecostalism

> The Holiness Movement traces its roots to John Wesley's insistence that Christians, in this life, might become perfect in love or intention. This teaching, and the experience known as "Christian perfection" or "entire sanctification" that grew out of it, found fertile ground in the perfectionistic climate of antebellum North America. By the late 1830s, three groups of closely related, but distinct bodies of perfectionists could be found, especially in the northern United States and Canada. They include Methodists, often associated with New York lay evangelist Phoebe Palmer; Oberlin perfectionist, often associated with Asa Mahan and Charles G. Finney; and the

54. Paulose, "Religionless Christianity."
55. Leibholz, "Memoir," in Bonhoeffer, *Cost of Discipleship*, 34.
56. Metaxas, foreword to Bonhoeffer, *Cost of Discipleship*, 6.

> so-called antinomian perfectionist, most notably associated with John Humphrey Noyes's Oneida community. The first two perfectionist denominations, the Wesleyan Methodist Church (1843) and the Free Methodist Church (1860), united features of Methodist perfectionism and Oberlin perfectionism.[57]

The Holiness Movement gave birth to a Christian revival in 1906 with a movement that is referred to as the Azusa Street Revival. The Azusa Street Revival was a historic, longstanding event born in Los Angeles, California, in the early twentieth century that played a significant role in the spread of Pentecostalism in America. William J. Seymour, an African American preacher, led it. It began with a meeting on April 14, 1906, and continued until roughly 1915.[58] This form of Christianity emphasizes spiritual gifts, mainly speaking in tongues, prophecy, and healing.

Pentecostalism established the black Holiness churches. The Church of God in Christ, founded by Bishop Charles Harrison Mason in 1907 in Memphis, Tennessee, is "presently the largest African-American Pentecostal church in the United States."[59]

"The Church of Christ (Holiness) U.S.A. was founded in 1896 by Charles Price Jones."[60] "JJ. Frazee founded the PAW in 1906 and was its first General Superintendent. At its founding it was a Charismatic movement with everyone enjoying the baptism of the Holy Spirit. The Oneness Pentecostal doctrine and liturgy of water baptism in Jesus' Name was not yet adopted."[61] "The Full Gospel Baptist Church Fellowship (FGBCF) or Full Gospel Baptist Church Fellowship International (FGBCFI) was founded by Bishop Paul Sylvester Morton in 1994."[62] "The United House of Prayer for All People, or United House of Prayer (UHOP), was

57. Kostlevy, *Historical Dictionary*, xiii.
58. Apostolic Archives International, "Azusa Street Revival."
59. COGIC, "Our Founder."
60. Alexander, *Black Fire*, 7–8.
61. PAW ECN West, "Our History."
62. Full Gospel Baptist Church, "Leadership."

founded by Marcelino Manuel da Graça, affectionately known as Charles Manuel 'Sweet Daddy' Grace, or Daddy Grace, in 1919."[63]

Established in 1992 in Atlanta, Georgia, the Conference of National Black Churches (CNBC) "represents more than 80% of African American Christians across this nation [with] a combined membership of over 20 million people and 30,000 congregations." Through the CNBC, member denominations work together to prioritize "health, social justice and public policy on behalf of African American communities."[64]

Estrelda Alexander's book *Black Fire: One Hundred Years of African American Pentecostalism* (2011) is a treasure of scholarly history on African American Pentecostalism. This book is significant because it chronicles the rich history of the black Pentecostal church and sheds knowledge on the tradition's diverse social and theological challenges. It tackles issues like the role of African Americans in Pentecostalism, slave religion or slave Christianity, race, and white racism. Additionally, Alexander explores the history of two failed experiments in interracialism: the Church of God in Christ under Charles Harrison Mason's leadership and the Pentecostal Assemblies of the World under the leadership of Garfield T. Hayward.[65] "In 1907, the Church of God in Christ, led by its black founder, C. H. Mason, was the only Pentecostal body chartered by the federal government to provide ministerial credentials."[66] Clergy were then able to receive benefits such as discounts on train fares and obtain conscientious objector status at the time of World War I. "So, at first white and black Pentecostal ministries sought credentialing with Mason."[67] Alexander also addresses the importance of "William Seymour and the Azusa Street revival and the role he played in founding American Pentecostalism."[68] She also discusses the historic role women,

63. Alexander, *Black Fire*, 21.

64. The Conference of National Black Churches (CNBC), "About."

65. Alexander, *Black Fire*, 8–9.

66. Alexander, *Black Fire*, 269.

67. Alexander, *Black Fire*, 269.

68. Alexander, *Black Fire*, 8.

such as "Bishops Mary Magdalena Tate and Ida Robinson," played in establishing the movement.[69] Alexander addresses sexism, gender, racism, and preaching that shaped and changed black Pentecostalism. Likewise, Cheryl J. Sanders's book *Saints in Exile: The Holiness-Pentecostal Experience in African-American Religion and Culture* (1996) addresses the Holiness and Pentecostal movements. It gives an overview of the spirituality of African American Christians in the United States from slavery to the present. It evaluates the impact of the Holiness and Pentecostal churches' impact on African Americans' culture and religious practices.

THE AFRICAN AMERICAN PROPHETIC PREACHER IN CONTEMPORARY AMERICA

The context of the African American preacher remains highly relevant in contemporary America. In the face of ongoing racial tensions, the African American preacher continues to serve as a moral compass and advocate for social justice. Growing up in the American South, Esau McCaulley experienced the constant struggle between despair and hope that characterizes the lives of some African Americans. In his book *Reading While Black: African American Biblical Interpretation as an Exercise in Hope*, he concludes that Bible reading and interpretation, as practiced in traditional black churches, are crucial elements in the fight for hope amid social injustice. Despite being often disregarded or viewed with suspicion by the wider church and academy, this ecclesial tradition holds something vital for today.

The sermons of African American preachers often draw from the Old Testament, especially the prophetic literature. Dr. Carter G. Woodson, a historian, author, and known as the "Father of Black History," writes, "The first real educators to take up the work of enlightening American Negroes were clergymen interested in the propagation of the gospel among the heathen in the new

69. Alexander, *Black Fire*, 9.

world."[70] The primary purpose of education was to convey to the black community the religious ideas and practices of the dominant culture. Dr. Kenyatta Gilbert explores African American prophetic rhetorical traditions relevant to all in his book *Exodus Preaching: Crafting Sermons About Justice and Hope* (2018). He understands the prophetic preaching of the prophets as a spoken word of justice for the diverse society. Gilbert stated that African American preachers draw heavily from the exodus story, Jesus' messianic witness, and prophetic literature to develop prophetic sermons. He also explains how preachers can effectively adapt their sermon preparation to address social change, racial unrest, and violence.

Gilbert remarks, "Exodus preaching (African American prophetic preaching) is concrete and daring discourse that names God and offers a vision of divine purpose."[71] He also identifies four key discourse features that can help in this process: "unmasking evil and dethroning idols,"[72] "confronting human tragedy and communal despair,"[73] "naming reality in a tone-deaf culture,"[74] and "inventive speech and poetic perceptions."[75] Gilbert believes using these strategies would allow the black preacher to see the bigger picture while mapping their message for exodus preaching.

Aaron Chalmers, PhD, is the head of the School of Ministry, Theology, and Culture at Tabor Adelaide. Tabor Adelaide is a multidenominational, evangelical college located in Adelaide, Australia. Chalmers specializes in teaching the Old Testament and hermeneutics. Moreover, he has published a book titled *Exploring the Religion of Ancient Israel: Prophet, Priest, Sage, and People* (2012). Chalmers is a biblical scholar determined to help preachers interpret the prophetic books deeply and meticulously by comparing and contrasting aspects of prophetism in our contemporary contexts with that of the prophets in the biblical world.

70. Woodson, *Education*, 18.
71. Gilbert, *Exodus Preaching*, 1.
72. Gilbert, *Exodus Preaching*, 17.
73. Gilbert, *Exodus Preaching*, 45.
74. Gilbert, *Exodus Preaching*, 67.
75. Gilbert, *Exodus Preaching*, 89.

In his brief section titled "What Is a Prophet? Modern Answers," Chalmers examines some of the major prophets that have contributed to the current state of American prophetic preaching and discusses several key issues and questions that effective prophetic preaching should confront. He quotes three powerful prophetic voices. One of those voices is the Reverend Dr. Martin Luther King Jr. and another is Marita Golden: "We knew no one man had killed the prophet. Rather, the combined weight of racism and an absence of moral courage had crushed him. A constitution ignored, laws denied, these were the weapons. America pulled the trigger."[76] Chalmers suggests that a prophet is viewed as a social reformer. This title could be applied to a political and social activist who seeks to bring about a change within their society. He notes, "In this case, the biblical prophets are viewed as early advocates of social justice and defenders of the marginalized."[77]

Leonora Tubbs Tisdale's book *Prophetic Preaching: A Pastoral Approach* (2010) tackles the question surrounding the (seeming) lack of prophetic witness in the church. Tisdale spends a reasonable amount of time analyzing others' definitions and concludes that prophetic preaching is the intersection of human suffering and God's proclaimed grace. Prophetic proclamation requires a heart that breaks for the things that break God's heart. It demands a passion for justice, imagination, courage, conviction to speak God's words, and humility and honesty in preaching.

Figures like Rev. Martin Luther King Jr., who emerged as a leading civil rights activist and preacher, symbolize the pivotal role of the African American preacher in advocating for justice. The social context in which African American preachers operate is marked by their ongoing struggles against racial inequality, economic disparities, and systemic discrimination. Their sermons often address these issues, offering their congregations solace, encouragement, and a call to action. Cleophus J. LaRue, in his book *I Believe I Will Testify* (2011), writes about the four essentials of preaching the Scriptures: "Four essentials come together in the

76. Golden, *Migrations of the Heart*, 14.

77. Chalmers, *Interpreting the Prophets*, 5.

best of black preaching. They are God, the scripture, the preacher, and the black lived experience."[78] When the black preacher is given an impartation from God through the Scriptures and can articulate the meaning of Scripture with his/her lived experience, it helps to move the people toward God's will for their lives. Therefore, sermons often addressed social justice.

To note another aspect of impact on American culture, African American preachers have contributed significantly to developing gospel music, a genre deeply rooted in the African American church experience. Gospel music has enriched the worship experience and profoundly influenced American music, giving birth to soul, R&B, and contemporary Christian music. Henry Mitchell writes, "Black preaching inherently depends on call and response. African music and oral communication are characterized by considerable audience participation."[79]

Returning to the issue of justice, the Black Lives Matter movement, which gained prominence recently, saw many African American preachers actively involved in protests and advocacy efforts. For example, the Reverend James Perkins, Dr. William Barber II, and Dr. Jamal H. Bryant were involved in the NAACP. The NAACP recently issued a travel warning for Florida in response to Governor DeSantis's legislative efforts to disregard black history and the programs that advocated for diversity, equity, and inclusion:

> Florida is openly hostile toward African Americans, people of color, and LGBTQ+ individuals. Before traveling to Florida, please understand that the state of Florida devalues and marginalizes the contributions of and the challenges faced by African Americans and other communities of color.[80]

Up until this point, I have only mentioned church-based social activists. Their faith gave them the resources to transcend the

78. LaRue, *I Believe I Will Testify*, loc. 57.

79. Mitchell, *Black Preaching*, loc. 30.

80. NAACP, "Travel Advisory."

brutality and still hope for a brighter future. It is truly a matter of grace that African Americans, after two and half centuries of slavery, another century of lynching, and Jim Crow segregation, can still love white people. In addition to the rise of the Black Power movement, which challenged the relevance of the black church, was the prominence of the Honorable Elijah Muhammad, the heir to the founder of the Nation of Islam (NOI), Wali Fard Muhammad, and the still popular voice of Malcolm X.

The NOI is a religious and political organization founded in Detroit, Michigan, in 1930 by Wali Fard Muhammad. After his mysterious disappearance in 1933, his successor, Elijah Poole, affectionately known as Elijah Muhammad, assumed the head of the NOI. His leadership produced two of the NOI's most excellent spokespeople: Malcolm X and Louis Farrakhan. According to Dawn-Marie Gibson, "The NOI finds its roots in Marcus Garvey's Universal Negro Improvement Association (UNIA) and Noble Drew Ali's Moorish Science Temple of America (MSTA)."[81]

Yet, the predominance of the African American prophetic preacher is unmistakable. African American preachers have expanded their reach beyond the pulpit through social media, radio, television, and the internet to spread their messages of hope, empowerment, and social change. Figures like Rev. Jessie Jackson, Rev. Al Sharpton, and Rev. Dr. Jamal H. Bryant show the modern-day influence of African American preachers in both religious and secular spheres. The context of the African American preacher is deeply rooted in a historical legacy of resilience and activism. They have navigated a complex social landscape marked by racial oppression, segregation, and racism, drawing strength from their faith and cultural heritage. Their role in advocating for civil rights and social justice remains paramount in contemporary American society.

The African American preacher remains a symbol of hope, a voice for the marginalized, and a catalyst for positive change in a nation grappling with racial inequality and oppression. Brian K. Blount, in his book *Then the Whisper Put on Flesh: New Testament*

81. Gibson, *History of the Nation of Islam*, 13.

Ethics in an African American Context, surmises that devastating circumstances still enslave most African Americans in American society today, especially in urban environments. They struggle with economic devastation, family disintegration, black-on-black crime, unemployment, and political and social injustice, as well as the structural racism that fuels all of these. Many black preachers are still pressing into the issues of justice; as Blount writes, "The Bible has always been read through the experience of the people holding it."[82]

Historically, African American preachers have played crucial roles in the fight for civil rights and social justice. This tradition continues today, with many missional pastors/preachers actively engaged in addressing issues such as racial inequality, economic injustice, and police brutality. Missional pastors use their platforms today to speak out against systemic oppression and advocate for positive change within their communities and society. In many cases, African American preachers serve as bridges between different segments of society, fostering dialogue and understanding across racial, ethnic, and religious lines. The African American preacher continues to be a dynamic and influential figure in contemporary America, profoundly shaping the spiritual, social, and cultural landscape.

82. Blount, *Then the Whisper*, 13.

CHAPTER THREE

AFRICAN AMERICAN EMBODIED JUSTICE PREACHING IN FLORIDA

THIS CHAPTER TURNS TO a historical overview of African American social justice preaching in Florida and reports on how preaching was embodied in the activism of the preacher. We have concluded that social justice preaching is rooted in a rich history of resilience, spirituality, and activism. The African American preacher's context is multifaceted and deeply interconnected with the broader African American experience. Furthermore, the chapter will highlight the significant historical events that formed and shaped African American social justice preaching in Florida; two critical personalities in the story of Florida and social change were the Reverend C. K. Steele and Father Pinder. These two giants in the faith led to change throughout Florida through the power of preaching.

FLORIDA AS A SANCTUARY

"The historic *Underground Railroad* of America which made legends of Harriet Tubman and Frederick Douglass was not located underground nor was it a railroad. A loose organised network with no clear, defined routes, the word *underground* relays the secrecy of the network's activities and the fear of exposure of slaves fleeing the hell of the confederate states."[1] In the late eighteenth century, many white Quakers began to actively assist enslaved African Americans in their quest for freedom. Their beliefs in justice, equality, and nonviolence compelled them to provide refuge and support to escaping slaves. The destination of the first or original Underground Railroad was not the North but the South, to Florida. Florida was the very first state in the Union to provide sanctuary for escaped slaves.

Over the course of roughly twenty-five years, Fort Mose, located just north of Spanish St. Augustine, functioned as a refuge for Africans escaping enslavement under English colonial rule during a broader imperial struggle among European powers in the Americas. Freedom at Fort Mose was contingent upon pledging loyalty to the Spanish crown and entering the Catholic faith. Historical estimates suggest that approximately one hundred Africans settled there. As historian Jane Landers notes, Fort Mose became "the first legally sanctioned free Black community in what is now the United States," and its residents formed a culturally dynamic society shaped by African traditions alongside Spanish, Native American, and English influences.[2] Fort Mose thus stands as an early example of black autonomy, cultural creativity, and negotiated freedom within the colonial Atlantic world.

Fort Mose was founded by a formerly enslaved person known as Francisco Menéndez. "Menéndez was an African-born slave who obtained freedom and became a militia captain, corsair, and co-founder of the first free black town in what would become the United States."[3] Fort Mose was established by the Spanish authorities in 1738, making it one of the earliest free black communities at the time. It was located about two miles north of St. Augustine, Florida. According to Kathleen A. Deagan, PhD, a research curator of archaeology and adjunct professor of anthropology and history at the University of Florida's Florida Museum of Natural History, and Jane Landers, PhD, author and Gertrude Conaway

1. Gabi-Williams, review of *The Underground Railroad.*
2. Landers, *Black Society in Spanish Florida*, 26.
3. Landers, "Francisco Menéndez."

Vanderbilt Professor of History and director of the Slave Societies Digital Archive at Vanderbilt University,

> Mose was born of the initiative and determination of Africans who, at great risk, manipulated the extended Anglo-Spanish conflict over the "debatable lands" between St. Augustine and Charleston to their own advantage. The community was composed of former slaves who escaped from British plantations and made their way south to Spanish Florida, where eventually they secured their freedom. That they became free was not unusual, for Spanish law and custom allowed many routes out of bondage, and free Africans had played active roles in Spain long before the voyages of Columbus. Africans were also critical to the exploration and settlement of the so-called New World, especially in the inhospitable coastal areas of the circum-Caribbean.[4]

"Harriet Tubman is perhaps the most well-known of all the Underground Railroad's 'conductors.' During a ten-year span, she made 19 trips into the South and escorted over 300 slaves to freedom. And, as she once proudly pointed out to Frederick Douglass, in all of her journeys she 'never lost a single passenger.'"[5] Tubman is one of the few women in the history of the United States who escaped slavery and has been celebrated as a hero who stood against the dominant culture's oppression and marginalization of black and brown people.

> Born Araminta Ross (and affectionately called "Minty") in March of 1822 to parents Harriet (Rit) Green Ross and Benjamin Ross, Tubman was one of nine children. The Ross family were enslaved in Dorchester County, Maryland. Chattel slavery determined that Black people were property that were bought and sold. The children of enslaved women were also considered enslaved, regardless of whether their fathers were enslaved or not. Such was the case for Tubman and her siblings as Benjamin was free, but Rit was not (University at Buffalo). The

4. Deagan and Landers, "Fort Mose," 265–66.

5. PBS, "Harriet Tubman."

> Ross' enslaver, Edward Brodess, did not allow the family to remain together and worked to split them up through the assignment of work. Separated from Benjamin Ross at a young age, Rit, Araminta and her siblings worked on a different farm owned by the Brodesses in Bucktown, Maryland.[6]

Both Menéndez and Tubman have done great things to fight and advocate for the fair and equal treatment of everyone in this country. Tubman was a very strong-willed woman with a great faith in God. "Historians now know that Tubman had narcolepsy," which is a neurological disorder that impairs a person's ability to regulate their sleep-wake cycles.[7] Tubman used what many would call a disability to guide her as she led many slaves to freedom. Not only should these two iconic figures be remembered and honored, but their commitment and dedication should be matched and continued by today's pastors, activists, and freedom fighters in the fight for justice, equity, and equality.

PREACHERS OF SOCIAL JUSTICE IN FLORIDA

Reverend Dr. Michael Evans, author and senior pastor of the Bethlehem Baptist Church in Mansfield, Texas, makes the following point in his book *Leadership in the Black Church: Guidance in the Midst of Changing Demographics*:

> Historically, the primary role model and person of prominence in the African American community was, for more than one hundred years, the pastor. He was the person looked upon by the community as the advocate for the rights of the people in his congregation. It was widely known that the Black pastor, after the abolition of slavery, was one of the few literate people in the community. Due to his value in the sight of the people as the chief spokesperson and spiritual guide of

6. Dawson, "Harriet Tubman."
7. Dawson, "Harriet Tubman."

> the community, people were encouraged to attend to the basic welfare of the pastor and his family.[8]

The pastor in the black church has long been the person looked upon to lead and advocate for the church and community. The Reverend Charles Kenzie, better known as "C. K." Steele (1914–1980), was a prominent African American pastor and civil rights leader known for his influential role in the Civil Rights Movement in Florida. Born on February 7, 1914, Steele was raised in the predominantly African American town of Gary, West Virginia, by his parents, Lyde Bailor and Henry L. Steele, a United States Steel and Coal Corporation miner.[9] Steele dedicated his life to advocating for racial equality, justice, social change, and improvement in the black community. He started preaching when he was fifteen and graduated from Morehouse College in 1938.

"Steele married Lois Marion Brock on January 14, 1941, in Montgomery, Alabama, and had six children."[10] Following his academic pursuits, he became a Baptist minister. He moved to Tallahassee, Florida, where he served as the pastor of Bethel Missionary Baptist Church for over fifty years and was president of the local NAACP chapter. Steele was elected president of the newly formed Inter-Civic Council (ICC) during the Tallahassee bus boycott.

One of Steele's most significant contributions to the Civil Rights Movement was his leadership in the Tallahassee bus boycott in 1956. This boycott followed the more famous Montgomery bus boycott and aimed to challenge racial segregation on public buses in Tallahassee. Steele's determination, charisma, and organizational skills played a crucial role in the boycott's success, ultimately leading to the end of segregated seating on city buses.

"Steele was also a dedicated supporter of the Southern Christian Leadership Conference (SCLC), an organization co-founded by the Rev. Dr. Martin Luther King Jr., Bayard Rustin, and other prominent civil rights leaders in Atlanta, Georgia, where he served

8. Evans, *Leadership in the Black Church*, loc. 519.

9. Stanford University, "Steele."

10. Padgett, "C. K. Steele," 26.

as the first vice president."[11] He also served as the SCLC's field director for Florida, organizing protests, voter registration drives, and various civil rights initiatives throughout the state.

Beyond his activism, Steele strongly advocated for education, housing, and economic opportunities for African Americans. He used his pulpit and involvement in the Civil Rights Movement to address these critical issues affecting his community. Throughout his life, Steele demonstrated unwavering commitment and courage in the face of racial discrimination and violence. His leadership and dedication helped pave the way for significant advancements in civil rights and social justice for African Americans in Florida. Sadly, Steele passed away from bone marrow cancer on August 19, 1980, but his legacy lives on as an enduring symbol of the struggle for equality and justice in America. His contributions continue to inspire future generations of pastors, preachers, activists, and advocates for civil rights.

The Reverend Canon Nelson Wardell Pinder, DD, was born in Miami (Overtown), Florida, on July 27, 1932, to the Reverend and Mrs. Pinder, where he grew up in the Liberty City Housing Project, commonly called "The Government Condos." Father Pinder is known as the "street priest," the "hoodlum's priest," a community leader, a caring person, a loving person, and your "priest and friend."[12] He was devoted to God, his fellow men, his wife, Marion, his family, his church, community, organizations, alma maters, Orange County, and Orlando, Florida. Following his family's tradition, Pinder enrolled in Bethune-Cookman College, in Daytona Beach, Florida. While at Bethune-Cookman College, he was drafted into the United States Army during the Korean War. After being honorably discharged, he returned to Bethune-Cookman, where he became active in student government and other campus groups. He graduated in 1956 with a degree in philosophy.

"Pinder then enrolled at Nashotah House Seminary in Nashotah, Wisconsin, to study and prepare himself for the priesthood and the Episcopal Church. In 1959, he was ordained into

11. Padgett, "C. K. Steele," 26.

12. Warren and MaultsBy, "Nelson W. Pinder."

the ministry and assigned to the Episcopal Church of Saint John the Baptist in Orlando. He married his college sweetheart, Marion Elizabeth Grant, on August 15, 1959."[13] An example of church involvement would be the influence and support of the Episcopalian church on Father Pinder during the Civil Rights Movement. "In the early 1960s, Pinder led high school students in sit-ins at Orlando restaurants and drug stores. He pushed for voting rights, desegregation, and equal pay for Black teachers."[14]

Many Southern black pastors and preachers were not educated but suffered through their personal experiences of racial discrimination throughout American society. One exception to the uneducated Southern preachers was the legendary Reverend Dr. Mack King Carter, a preacher par excellence and pastor emeritus of the New Mount Olive Baptist Church of Fort Lauderdale, Florida. "His extraordinary exegetical gift, brilliant mind, and masterful expertise in homiletics and hermeneutics earned him the title 'The Pastor's Pastor.'"[15]

> A native of Ocala, where he first became involved in ministerial work as a child, Carter was an accomplished theological academic and a dynamic speaker. He discussed the relationship between his roles as an instructor and a recruiter during his farewell sermon, given at his retirement just four years ago. Carter said that "preaching is for unbelievers" and, conversely, teaching is for believers.[16]

Another notable scholarly preacher from Florida was the Reverend Dr. Howard Washington Thurman. Thurman was a prominent African American theologian, author, educator, and civil rights leader. He was born in Daytona Beach, Florida, at a time when racial segregation and discrimination were deeply embedded within American society. Thurman was valedictorian

13. From a handout of a biography of Pinder created and given to me by the Episcopal Church of Saint John the Baptist, Orlando, Florida, June 2019.

14. Byrnes, "Episcopal Priest."

15. Osgood, "Our Founder."

16. Beatty, "South Florida Says Goodbye."

of his high school class and attended Morehouse College in Atlanta, Georgia, where he was mentored by the renowned scholar and civil rights leader Benjamin Mays. After graduating from Morehouse, Thurman continued his education at the Rochester Theological Seminary and then at Haverford College, where he pursued postgraduate studies at Haverford, earning a doctorate in theology. Thurman's writings focused on the connection between spirituality and social justice. He emphasized the importance of nonviolent resistance and the role of religion in promoting racial equality. His book *Jesus and the Disinherited*, published in 1949, remains a pivotal work on social justice. In it, he explored the relevance of Jesus' teachings to the struggles of marginalized and oppressed African American communities. Thurman played a significant role in the Civil Rights Movement in America.

He was a mentor and spiritual advisor to many prominent civil rights leaders, including Rev. Dr. Martin Luther King Jr. His philosophy of nonviolence and his emphasis on the dignity and worth of every individual helped shape the moral and ethical framework of Dr. King and the broader American Civil Rights Movement. "The Church for the Fellowship of All Peoples was founded in 1944 by Dr. Howard Thurman and Dr. Alfred Fisk as the nation's first interracial, interfaith congregation, and for over 75 years, the church has helped people to discover God's purpose for their lives."[17]

The late Reverend Dr. Olin P. Moyd made important observations about the importance of Thurman's preaching. Moyd was the author of two books, *The Sacred Art: Preaching and Theology in the African American Tradition* (1995) and *Redemption in Black Theology* (1979), along with numerous articles. He was the pastor of Mount Lebanon Baptist Church in Baltimore, Maryland, for forty years. Dr. Moyd examines the African American preaching tradition and contends that it has been the medium by which black theology has been expressed in African American assemblies. Preachers have proclaimed and interpreted the word of God, and

17. The Church for the Fellowship of All Peoples, "About Us."

their preaching has been "the hallmark of hope and the pivot of promise for a pilgrim people."[18] In chapter 1, Moyd writes,

> These truths were first proclaimed by the late Mystic, scholar, and theologian Howard Thurman at the annual convocation on preaching at the School of Theology, Boston University, in 1935. The title of the lecture was "Good News for the Disinherited." The disinherited of which Thurman spoke were the African Americans who had been disenfranchised by the majority of the Euro-Americans who claimed to be predominantly Christians. The context of Euro-American theology and preaching had little to say to those whose backs were against the wall. Nevertheless, the interpretations and proclamations of the gospel and African-American churches gave special attention to the conditions and aspirations of the people who were denied the fulfillment of the American dream of liberty and Justice for all.[19]

Black preachers in Florida who took the bold stand to preach social justice from their pulpits and, with their embodied preaching, their life sermons, were the moral and biblical compass of an oppressed people. The black pastor stands behind his sacred desk to confront racial injustices, redlining, residential segregation, unfair housing policies, sexism, discrimination, and a social caste system that constantly treats blacks like second-class citizens. Michael LeFebvre, pastor, writes, "Racial integration was the first social revolution which the Gospel brought to the New Testament world. And the New Testament presents interracial communion as one of the hallmarks of the redeemed in Christ."[20] It is important to note that the first-century church ushered in racial integration, which is a trademark of the Savior who redeems.

18. Moyd, *Sacred Art*, 1.

19. Moyd, *Sacred Art*, 1.

20. LeFebvre, "Neither Jew Nor Gentile," 33.

CHAPTER FOUR

CASE STUDIES FOR EXAMINATION

IN THIS SECTION, I will reintroduce the terms *constructivism* and *critical theory* and present the findings drawn from interviews. I asked questions about the significant role that African American preachers played and continue to play in advocating for social justice in Florida and throughout the United States. The goal was to identify the challenges preachers face and continue to face in addressing these issues in their preaching. Additionally, I aimed to understand how African American preachers gauge the effectiveness of their preaching on social justice issues.

Again, *constructivism* is a learning theory that holds that knowledge is best gained through reflection and active construction in the mind. Thus, knowledge is an intersubjective interpretation. The learner must consider the information being taught and construct an interpretation based on past experiences, personal views, and cultural background. Therefore, constructivism suggests that learners construct their understanding and knowledge of the world through experiencing and reflecting on those experiences.

Critical theory asserts that "reality may be objective, but competing groups continually contest truth."[1] *Lived experience* refers to individuals' personal, subjective experiences within their social

1. Swinton and Mowat, *Practical Theology*, loc. 71.

and cultural contexts. The use of interviews is considered ethnography. They were used to capture the personal experiences of the black preachers. The lived experience highlights the importance of centering the voices and perspectives of marginalized African Americans whose lived experiences differ from the dominant narratives. For example, whites do not have the lived experience of driving while black and brown simply because there is no lived experience of driving while white. A simple traffic stop for a black person could quickly turn tragic. At the same time, whites have the privilege of expressing their anger and outrage for being pulled over by the police. Earlier in this book, the neutrality of many black pastors on the issues of social justice was mentioned. The fact is that there are challenges faced by the African American preacher; there is a risk of being ostracized, arrested, and even killed for standing up against racism, sexism, and injustice. One of the questions this book explores and answers is, Is the risk of preaching on social justice issues perceived too great in our contemporary context?

First, experience impacts biblical interpretation. An important voice on the topic of black experience and biblical readings is Cain Hope Felder, PhD (1943–2019). He served as a New Testament language and literature professor at Howard University's School of Divinity from 1981 until his retirement in 2016. His book, *Stony the Road We Trod: African American Biblical Interpretation* (1991), is a hallmark of American black religion. Its distinctive reporting of the Bible has played a significant role in creating communities, resisting oppression, and promoting liberation, hope, and faithful engagement with God's redemptive work in history.

What can the African American experience with the Bible teach critical biblical studies, and vice versa? This remarkable volume highlights the emergence of a group of black biblical scholars who offer sophisticated exegesis, bringing together their unique experiences and perspectives. With a particular examination of biblical authority, the scholarly collection explores race, class, and gender sensitivities. Including African characters in biblical stories and the empowering messages found within Scripture revolutionizes how the church and academia interpret and apply the Bible to current societal issues. This shift in perspective is helping to redefine the questions, concerns, and scholarly approaches used to understand the role of the Bible in today's world, especially the world of the black preacher.

There are many challenges the African American preacher must face in the fight for freedom and equality, including the risk of being ostracized, arrested, and even killed for standing up against racism, sexism, and injustice. Many preachers and politicians who stood up for social justice have been killed: President John F. Kennedy, Medgar Evers, Malcolm X, Robert Kennedy, and Rev. Dr. Martin Luther King Jr., to name a few. Many church-based social activists and black pastors feared white mob violence and lynching for speaking out against racism and injustice. An Equal Justice Initiative report "documents more than 4,440 racial terror lynchings in the United States" from 1877 to 1950.[2]

Mary Church Terrell was one of the first African American women to earn a college degree and became a national activist for civil rights and suffrage. She served as a Latin instructor at the M Street School in Washington, DC, the nation's first public high school established for African Americans. Terrell writes in her article "The Lynching from a Negro's Point of View," "Before 1904 was three months old, thirty-one negroes had been lynched."[3] Terrell informs the reader immediately that the lynching of black negroes was problematic. Terrell also explains that the killing of negroes by hangings and shootings was so common that it did not evoke "slight comments."[4]

Terrell further explains many whites who were aware of the lynchings refused to speak out against this cruel and barbaric practice committed by white mobs against black people to satisfy their thirst for "mob justice."[5] Terrell attempts to understand the root causes of lynching and the social sensation it created among

2. Equal Justice Initiative, "Lynching in America."
3. Terrell, "Lynching," 853.
4. Terrell, "Lynching," 853.
5. Terrell, "Lynching," 853.

white Southerners. Pertaining to lynching, Terrell writes, "Four mistakes are commonly made." Terrell explains, "In the first place, it is a great mistake to suppose that rape is the real cause of lynching in the South."[6]

Second, Terrell states that following emancipation, African Americans endured sustained violence that was largely organized and systematic, perpetrated primarily by the Ku Klux Klan and other coordinated vigilante groups. Third, Terrell writes, "It is easy to prove that rape is simply the pretext and not the cause of lynching."[7] Finally, Terrell writes about what was then socially acceptable behavior for Southern whites and how Northern whites looked on with false pretenses of black and white relations in the South.

A prime example of white mob violence and lynching happened in Ocoee, Florida, a town located right outside of Orlando. The Ocoee Massacre occurred on November 2, 1920, in Ocoee during the 1920 presidential election. It was one of the deadliest instances of election-day violence in United States history. "Mose Norman, a Black laborer, . . . arrived at the polls in the City of Ocoee in Orange County with other Black people attempting to vote." After twice being refused entry, he then had to flee attacks from armed white men. He hid at the home of his friend, Julius "July" Perry, a black farmer and civil rights leader who, like Norman, "worked to register Black residents in Orange County to vote." However, Norman was followed there by a mob, and Perry's home was burned down in their efforts to capture Norman. While Norman was able to escape, the mob instead had Perry arrested and beaten in jail. "The next day, [Perry] was lynched and shot."[8]

"An unknown number of African American citizens were murdered, and their homes and community were burned to the ground. Most of the Black population of Ocoee fled, never to return."[9]

6. Terrell, "Lynching," 853–54.
7. Terrell, "Lynching," 853–54.
8. ACLU Florida, "Remembering Ocoee."
9. Orange County Regional History Center, "Yesterday, This Was Home."

Like many towns across America, Ocoee was a "sundown town," according to James W. Loewen, author, racial justice activist, and professor who taught race relations for over twenty years at the University of Vermont. He previously taught at the predominantly black Tougaloo College in Mississippi. "A sundown town is any organized jurisdiction that for decades kept African Americans or other groups from living in it and was thus 'all-white' on purpose."[10] For blacks and minorities, this meant they should be out of town by sundown, or they would face the threat of lynching. Loewen also writes,

> Beginning in about 1890 and continuing until 1968, white Americans established thousands of towns across the United States for whites only. Many towns drove out their black populations, then posted sundown signs. Other towns passed ordinances barring African Americans after dark or prohibiting them from owning or renting property; still others established such policies by informal means, harassing and even killing those who violated the rule. Some Sundown towns similarly kept out Jews, Chinese, Mexicans, Native Americans, or other groups.[11]

"July Perry had become the well-respected godfather of the Black community. He served as a deacon in the church and the local labor leader or 'straw boss.'"[12] "Some African Americans speculated that the rioting may have been planned so that some whites could seize the property of the wealthiest Blacks in the town."[13] This was black voter suppression in action. This is what Carol Elaine Anderson, PhD, author and the Charles Howard Candler Professor of African American Studies at Emory University in Atlanta, Georgia, writes about in her book titled *White Rage: The Unspoken Truth of Our Racial Divide*. Anderson writes,

10. Loewen, *Sundown Towns*, 4.
11. Loewen, *Sundown Towns*, 4.
12. Zinn Education Project, "Ocoee Massacre."
13. Momodu, "Ocoee Massacre."

> The trigger for white rage, inevitably, is black advancement. It is not the mere presence of black people that is the problem; rather, it is blackness with ambition, with drive, with purpose, with aspirations, and with demands for full and equal citizenship. It is blackness that refuses to accept subjugation, to give up. A formidable array of policy assaults and legal contortions has consistently punished black resilience, black resolve.[14]

Anderson defines white rage as follows: "White rage is subtle as policymakers and a series of courts systematically undercut advancement of African Americans, and in doing so wreak major havoc on American democracy."[15] White rage is just violent acts committed by white mobs or the Ku Klux Klan (KKK).

In his book *The Color of Law: A Forgotten History of How Our Government Segregated America* (2017), Richard Rothstein explores the systemic and deliberate role that government policies played in segregating American cities and communities along racial lines. He argues that segregation was not merely the result of individual prejudices or economic disparities but rather the consequence of explicit government actions such as redlining, racially restrictive housing covenants, and discriminatory zoning laws.

> The federal government pursued two important policies in the mid-20th century that segregated metropolitan areas. One was the first civilian public housing program which frequently demolished integrated neighborhoods in order to create segregated public housing. The second program that the federal government pursued was to subsidize the development of suburbs on a condition that they be only sold to white families and that the homes in those suburbs had deeds that prohibited resale to African-Americans. These two policies worked together to segregate metropolitan areas in ways that they otherwise would never have been segregated.[16]

14. Anderson, *White Rage*, 3–4.
15. Emory University News Center, "Anderson Explores."
16. Rothstein, "Color of Law."

Rothstein writes, "We said they are '*de facto* segregated,' that they result from private practices, not from law or government policy."[17] Rothstein brings to light both "*de facto* segregation," which is private prejudices or discrimination, and "*de jure* segregation," which is "segregation by intentional government action" or "segregation by law and public policy."[18] Rothstein later writes, "Both public policy discrimination and societal discrimination express what these scholars term 'structural racism,' which many if not most institutions in the country operate to the disadvantage of African Americans."[19] All of these—*de facto*, *de jure*, and structural racism—have been powerful tools in the dominant culture's playbook for widening the economic gap between whites and blacks and ensuring black Americans stay second-class citizens in this country.

The African American missional pastor must still use his or her voice to speak out against structural racism in Florida today. Attorney Benjamin L. Crump is a civil rights lawyer and author; he writes in his book *Open Season: Legalized Genocide of Colored People*,

> This genocide is fueled by police brutality, unfair treatment in the judicial system, and stand-your-ground and shoot-first laws, which are influenced by the gun lobby. I show how those laws have contributed to and have too often justified the killing of people of color by private, mostly white male citizens or police.[20]

CONVERSATIONS WITH TODAY'S SOCIAL JUSTICE PREACHERS

The Reverend Dr. Carl Johnson, president of the Florida General Baptist Convention, appointed the Reverend Dr. R. B. Holmes Jr.,

17. Rothstein, *Color of Law*, vii.
18. Rothstein, *Color of Law*, viii.
19. Rothstein, *Color of Law*, xv.
20. Crump, *Open Season*, loc. 15.

senior pastor of the historic Bethel Missionary Baptist Church in Tallahassee, Florida, to chair the "Task Force Symposium: Crafting New Black History Curriculum" at Bethel, from February 24–25, 2024. "The purpose of the conference is two-fold: To highlight Black history and to present a proposed curriculum to the governor's office."[21]

Several media outlets interviewed three of the pastors assigned to the task force—Rev. Dr. R. B. Holmes Jr., Rev. Dr. Robert Spooney (senior pastor of the oldest black church in Orlando, the historic Mount Zion Institutional Baptist Church, and general secretary of the Florida General Baptist Convention), and Rev. Dr. Johnny Turner (author, former educator, and retired pastor)—following the close of the symposium. "The conference was planned in response to an 'attempt to distort and water down' Black history lessons in classrooms. Holmes spoke out and protested DeSantis' anti-woke agenda in the spring in Tallahassee after the governor effectively banned the College Board's AP African American History course and revised the state's Black history curriculum standards in 2023."[22] Holmes told the *Tallahassee Democrat*,

> We will present to the governor of Florida, the Commissioner of Education and the Board of Education a factual, accurate and correct teaching of African American history in our public schools. . . . An enslaved people didn't derive any benefits from slavery; slavery was brutal, treacherous, sinful and unscrupulous.[23]

The task force concluded their meeting with a prayer by the Reverend Dr. Robert Spooney:

> We lift up our governor and the head of this department of education, Mr. Diaz. . . . We ask God that you would touch their hearts, that you will move on them, that you will allow your spirit to enter them, that they will receive the documentation that has been presented, (that) they will digest it, decipher it, and then understand that it is

21. Brown, "Rev. R. B. Holmes."
22. Brown, "Rev. R. B. Holmes."
23. Brown, "Rev. R. B. Holmes."

> information that is accurate. The narrative, Lord, as you know, has not been changed, it has been corrected.[24]

Dr. Spooney is quoted on *Capital Outlook*'s website as saying,

> The fight for social justice and educational parity is an ongoing battle. The dismantling of programs of diversity, equity, and inclusion within our state and throughout this nation is an insult. We must not remain silent. I encourage you to assist in this effort as we continue to speak "Truth to Power." To quote Frederick Douglass, "We are one, our cause is one and we must help each other if we are to succeed."[25]

The Revered Dr. Johnny Turner also writes in the *Capital Outlook*, "The Governor of the State of Florida aims to remove our history from the Florida State Educational Curriculum. As a member of The Task Force, our Initiative is inherently significant to defend our rich history as African Americans. During slavery, our forefathers and mothers did not benefit from slavery, but utilized their skills meaningfully. We aim to maintain our history for generations to come."[26] I concur with these powerful preachers. We must not be silent but should speak out against this vicious attack on our history and ensure that our history is being properly taught in school.

Interview 1: Rev. Dr. R. B. Holmes Jr.[27]

The Reverend Dr. R. B. Holmes Jr. is the pastor of the historic Bethel Missionary Baptist Church in Tallahassee, Florida. The church is located in the heart of downtown Tallahassee, Florida's Frenchtown community. Bethel Missionary Baptist Church was established in

24. Goñi-Lessan, "Faith Leaders."
25. Spooney, "Freedom Schools."
26. *Capital Outlook*, "Teaching Our Own History."
27. Due to limited space here, the researcher was not able to capture all the ethnographic information from all the interviews. See appendix A for all those who participated in this research.

1870. Dr. Holmes has served faithfully for thirty-three years of his nearly four decades in pastoral leadership at the Bethel Missionary Baptist Church. His mission continues to be to "transform people for the glory of God and the good of the community."[28] Dr. R. B. Holmes has been recognized locally, across the state, and nationally for his outstanding contributions. He is a pastor who is fully supported by his congregation of over three thousand members.

Dr. Holmes has led the transformation of the Frenchtown community. He has been appointed to various university boards of trustees and statewide policy-making bodies by five Florida governors. Dr. R. B. Holmes is highly respected across the country and has provided stellar leadership in major faith-based organizations, including the National Baptist Convention, USA, Inc., the National Action Network, and the National Save the Family Now Movement, Inc., of which he is president and founder.[29] The Bethel Baptist Church was identified by the Casey Family Programs as a "Community of Hope," bringing national exposure to the church. Dr. Holmes's extensive training and breadth of experience have equipped him with significant conceptual, technical, and relational expertise that continue to benefit the church. In September 2016, he was honored with the prestigious Lifetime Leadership Award by the Tallahassee Chamber of Commerce in recognition of his exceptional and enduring contributions. Grounded in the values instilled by his late parents, Deacon R. B. Holmes Sr. and Sister Lucille Holmes, Dr. Holmes remains deeply committed to family. He approaches his roles as husband, father, brother, grandfather, and uncle with seriousness and integrity. Dr. Holmes has been married to Dr. Gloria P. Holmes for more than thirty-two years. As he often affirms, "To God be the glory for the great and wonderful things he has done."[30]

> *Researcher*: Dr. Holmes, can you tell me your name and a little bit about your background?

28. Bethel Missionary Baptist Church, "Rev. Dr. R. B. Holmes."
29. Bethel Missionary Baptist Church, "Rev. Dr. R. B. Holmes."
30. See Bethel Missionary Baptist Church, "Rev. Dr. R. B. Holmes."

Dr. Holmes: I am R. B. Holmes Jr., the pastor of the Bethel Missionary Baptist Church in Tallahassee, Florida. I have been pastoring Bethel for thirty-eight years. I came there in 1986 from Jacksonville, where I pastored for ten years at the First Timothy Baptist Church from 1976 to 1986. As I stated, I came to Bethel in 1986 by the grace of God, and I have been there ever since. Bethel Missionary Baptist Church is a very historic church. As a matter of fact, it is the hallmark of black history. One of the major leaders was the former pastor, the Reverend C. K. Steele, who stayed there for twenty-nine years. He and the great Martin Luther King Jr. were cofounders in the late fifties of the Southern Christian Leadership Conference [SCLC]. Reverend Steele at Bethel led the sit-in boycotts in the city of Tallahassee in 1956. For almost 366 days African Americans refused to ride the city bus until they integrated the system. The same process and methodology took place under King's leadership in Montgomery, Alabama, at the Dexter Avenue Baptist Church. I think that my early upbringing kind of prophetically prepared me to hopefully become a pastor who had a strong sense for social justice, diversity, equity, and inclusion. I say that because, you know, when I finished my formal education, getting my doctorate from Virginia Union in the early nineties, the idea was to develop a curriculum around developing African American schools. So, we have Bethel Christian Academy, and it's been alive for now thirty-two years of operation, and this year, we are transitioning into an all-male academy.

I said that because at my undergraduate way back then at Malone University, I majored in sociology and went to college on a baseball scholarship when I finished at William M. Raines High School in Jacksonville, Florida, in 1968. Think about that: 1968 was the year that Dr. King was assassinated; 1965 there about was Malcolm X; and 1963, Medgar Evers. In the sixties. Fast forward, you were grounded in the understanding that the pulpit must teach people to go from the pulpit to the pavement to address the aches and pains and scars and bruises of our people. That came about because of systemic racism. If you keep a people in captivity and enslave them for four hundred years and work them without a paycheck and brutalize and beat them and damage them. We need reparations, restitution, and reconciliation.

So, back there in seminary, I knew that going to an all-white seminary, Methodist Theological Seminary in Delaware, Ohio, began to frame my mindset about the power of social justice. That's when I began to sense a calling to preach the gospel of Jesus Christ. Understanding where you are in a setting talking about white theology and not black theology, white nationalism and not black nationalism. You studied Malcolm X, Marcus Garvey, Nelson Mandela, MLK Jr., Medgar Evers, and Elijah Muhammad. You need to understand the master Jesus was a Savior who came to set the captors free. And to tell the oppressors if you know the truth, the truth will set you free. That kind of evolved and developed my who's-ness and sense of purpose. Which meant that I could not lead a church trying to get folks ready for heaven, and they lived like hell down here.

That's bad theology. So, my training morally and academically, my upbringing in Jacksonville, Florida, in a nice black middle-class neighborhood where everybody had a daddy in the house, where everybody had a sense of pride—my teachers, preachers, doctors, and dentists all lived in the same neighborhood. All the people were named after strong African Americans like Larry Doby, Jackie Robinson, Marcus Garvey, Malcolm X, and A. Phillip Randolph, so you know, Brother Montgomery, man, coming up, you're thinking about that. I lived on Campanella Drive named after Roy Campanella. Every street in the neighborhood was named after a black person. If you look back over the years at all, that was ingrained in you at an early age. I went to a high school where my principal said, "We are somebody." I learned early on from Jesse Jackson the slogan "I am somebody." So that framed my theology.

Fast forward to formal education, a terminal degree from Virginia Union, coming through and living black history in real time, and studying leading abolitionists and civil rights leaders, and leaders of the period of Reconstruction and periods prior to that. You cannot become a preacher who is scared of Pharoah or Hitler in the twenty-first century. You cannot become afraid of these wrong-winged Republicans who try to turn back the hands of time as they did in the 1800s, when the Republican party, which was against slavery, is now moving a decade forward, and the Republican, which has changed to be a party of white nationalism, Jim Crow-ism, and against diversity, equity, and inclusion. Which leads me back to where I am today. You cannot allow a governor or anybody to say that your education, black history, lacks educational value. You cannot give anyone a pass who says that blacks benefited from slavery. Breaking news: the only people who benefitted from slavery were the slave masters, and they are still benefitting from slavery today.

Researcher: Dr. Holmes, what impact do you believe that preachers had prior to the Civil Rights Movement in the state of Florida within the community concerning race?

Dr. Holmes: Remember I mentioned C. K. Steele, who pastored Bethel for twenty-nine in the fifties and passed in the late eighties. The founder of Bethel church was an enslaved man from Virginia who they brought him to Tallahassee. He started Bethel in 1870. Father James Page started a school, an elementary school in the 1870s. He became the first black county commissioner in the 1800s. Also, from Bethel, he started the oldest association, the First Bethlehem Association. The First Bethlehem Association was birthed at Bethel under the leadership of James Page. He was the first pastor of the Bethel Missionary Baptist Church in Tallahassee, and then from the first association, Father Page and his group started the Florida General Baptist Convention. From the Florida General Baptist Convention started Florida College, which is now Florida Memorial University, and from that convention started the Foreign Mission Board that became the National Baptist Convention USA Incorporated. So, Bethel is rooted and grounded in social justice, and its founder, a former slave, learned how to read and write and used his skills to impact politics, education, economics, and the religious communities across this state and across this country. Those preachers back in the Reconstruction period had vision, courage, and tenacity, and they were not afraid to die.

Researcher: Dr. Holmes, how have African American preachers influenced social movements like the Civil Rights Movement, and how has preaching influenced the passing of legislation on social justice, such as the Voter's Rights and the Civil Rights Act?

Dr. Holmes: Remember now, the Civil Rights Movement was birthed in the black church. Dr. King was a black Baptist preacher who started the Civil Rights Movement, who dealt with police brutality, segregation in public accommodations, in schools, sports arenas, you name it. Remember, it was the pastors and their members who led the Civil Rights Movement. Why? Because the pastors were the freest voices in that community. Because he/she received their salary from the hands, hearts, and souls of black people. Any black pastor who was pastoring full-time had a sense of urgency to do what Dr. King talked about to build a "Beloved Community." Therefore, the Civil Rights Acts of 1964, the Voters Rights Act of 1965, and the Fair Housing Act of 1968 were all birthed through the Civil Rights Movement. The Civil Rights Movement became the Student Nonviolent Coordinating Committee [SNCC] and the Congress of Racial Equality [CORE]. It was those black pastors who started schools in their basements in the 1800s. Most of your historically black colleges and universities [HBCUs] came out of the black church, came through pastors informing their congregations that we need to educate our people. Remember, during that time it was illegal for blacks to read and write. If you found a slave who could read and write, they would be lynched before sundown. When you talk about our history, black history, I am very adamant about not letting anyone water down or erase our history or delete or dilute our history. We are moving out of righteous indignation and on what Ron Penning says, "Listen to the blood." You cannot listen to the blood if you don't understand who shed that blood. These preachers today, and those from the 1800s

> and the Civil Rights Movement—listen, Dr. King did not die because of cancer. He died from the cancer of racism. He was assassinated because he stood up for what was right and righteousness. Malcolm X did not die because he ate too much pork. He died because he understood that he was somebody, and he understood the power of black nationalism. Medgar Evers did not die playing football. He died for the right to vote. He was shot at his own home in his driveway. Because the KKK said, you're doing too much trying to use the pulpit and the NAACP to mobilize voters to vote. John Lewis on the Edman Pettus Bridge, his skill was almost knocked out. Because he was not on a fishing vacation or on a cruise, but he was cruising, walking across that Edman Pettus Bridge. It was all undergirded morally by the Civil Rights Movement led by black pastors and lay people. Without the black church, there would be no Civil Rights Movement.[31]

Reflection on Interview 1: Rev. Dr. R. B. Holmes Jr.

Dr. Holmes offers more than a historical account—he embodies a legacy of prophetic resistance and community transformation. His commitment to education, political engagement, and theological formation reveals a holistic pastoral identity that refuses to separate salvation from social transformation. His insistence that "bad theology" is trying to prepare people for heaven while ignoring their hellish conditions on earth captures the very heart of embodied social justice preaching. His experiences with white theological institutions, his grounding in black history, and his connection to icons like C. K. Steele and MLK all demonstrate that black preaching must never be disembodied from the struggle for justice.

What stands out significantly is Holmes's emphasis on place—Jacksonville and Tallahassee are not just cities but contexts that shaped his prophetic voice. His rejection of sanitized Christianity compels today's preachers to revisit the pulpit's purpose, especially in the face of erasure and revisionist history. He models how the

31. From the author's interview of Dr. Holmes.

black preacher can be both a scholar and an activist, deeply rooted in the past while contending for justice in the present. His leadership reminds us that embodied social justice preaching is not a trend but a theological necessity for communities still fighting to be seen, heard, and healed.

Interview 2: Rev. Dr. Arthur Sims Sr.

Reverend Dr. Arthur Sims Sr. was on the front lines during the Civil Rights Movement and has been a social justice preacher and activist for over sixty years. Dr. Sims is the founder and senior pastor of the Fellowship Baptist Church of Pine Hills, located in Orlando, Florida, and a church-based activist of the Civil Rights Movement era. Dr. Sims Sr. was born March 22, 1944, in Oglethorpe County, Maxeys, Georgia, to Rev. James H. Sims Sr. and Sarah E. Sims. His father was a legendary pastor, and his mother was a gifted singer. Being the second of six children, he came from a very close-knit family. Reverend Sims gave his life to Christ at the age of five by uniting with Oconee Baptist Church and was baptized by the Reverend J. C. Williams. For the first nine years of his life, he was raised on a 162-acre farm and thereby knew the discipline of farm life. His mother prepared him well for school as he entered Oconee Elementary School at the age of five and began his studies in the second grade. At Oconee, he soon became known for his gift of singing and academic achievement.

At the age of nine, the family moved to Athens, Georgia, where he enrolled in the Union

Baptist Institute, a private Baptist school that functioned alongside the public educational system for African Americans during segregation. His family became part of the Ebenezer Baptist Church West under the leadership of Rev. J. C. Sanders. At Ebenezer, he led the youth choir. He soon enrolled at Athens High Industrial School, where he was a soloist for the school's chorus and graduated as an honor student and ranked number five in his class of 105.

He received the Principal's Award from Professor H. T. Edwards in music. Dr. Sims was taught to sing and was influenced greatly in music by his teachers: the Reverend W. F. Billups, Professor H. T. Edwards, and Mrs. Carrie Billups. In 1961, he enrolled at Paine College in Augusta, Georgia, where he received a bachelor of arts degree with a major in history and a minor in philosophy of religion. While at Paine, he excelled in music, receiving voice training from Dr. Emily Remington, Ms. Porter Remington, and Ms. Ruby Jenkins.

Dr. Sims was called to pastor the Crossroad Baptist Church in Washington, Georgia, at the age of eighteen, and at the age of nineteen, he became the pastor of the First Mt. Moriah Baptist Church in Augusta. The Mt. Moriah Baptist Church was rebuilt under his leadership and became a persuasive force in the Augusta community. While pastoring in Augusta, he attended Morehouse School of Religion under the auspices of the Interdenominational Theological Center (ITC), of Atlanta. As a student at ITC, he led the student government and graduated with a master of divinity degree (MDiv). He also received the Malthalathian Award for having the highest grade point average for Morehouse School of Religion.

In 1966, he married Jeanne Gloria Stephens Sims (now deceased). Four children were born into this union. Pastor Sims was a gospel radio host for WAUG radio station. Later, he became a high school teacher at Blanchard High School while completing further studies at Augusta College (University). Pastor Sims became a leader in civil rights and maintained two broadcast ministries. In addition to pastoring and being a civil rights leader, he became the executive director of the Community Development Project, a Rust DuPont Poverty Program. Dr. Sims said, "I am a country boy, a country preacher out of Maxeys in Athens, Georgia. I have pastored for sixty-two years, and singing gives me joy."[32]

> *Researcher*: Dr. Sims, how did the black preachers impact the church and community before the Civil Rights Movement?

32. From the author's interview of Dr. Sims.

Dr. Sims: I believe black pastors have always had an influence and impact on everything that black folks have done, even before the Civil Rights Movement. I believe that black pastors have always influenced the culture; pastors have influenced participation in singing, doing freedom protest marches and sit-ins, influencing, and encouraging home ownership, or whatever business ownership, whatever little savings account black folks had. His words [the words of the pastor] meant a lot, and he influenced their behavior. Perhaps when he spoke. People believed him. The issue of influence was quite great, whether it was good or bad.

Researcher: Dr. Sims, how have the African American preachers influenced the Civil Rights Movement in Florida and nationwide?

Dr. Sims: The NAACP was started by black pastors. The Civil Rights Movement was started by black pastors and the black church. For some reason, the whites respected the black church and did not invade it. The black pastor was courageous, and there were a lot of black pastors who were against the black pastors being a part of the Civil Rights Movement. The black pastors in the Civil Rights Movement, most notably Dr. King, were tremendous in particular with their speeches, oratory, and in keeping people together and fired up so that we would not lose track as to what we should be doing.

Researcher: Dr. Sims, how have African American preachers influenced the Civil Rights Movement and the passing of legislation on civil rights?

Dr. Sims: I don't think it was because of the influence of black pastors that these bills and legislation was passed. I think the black pastors and preachers have helped to pave the way and encouraged and motivated politicians. Politicians have always depended on the black pastor, preacher, and morticians to get other people in the church moving, to get the community moving. Pastors and morticians have always had a great influence on the community. In fact, most black politicians were members of the black church and were influenced by a black pastor. Let me put it this way: C. K. Steele was "A Man of Steel," and he was fearless! He spoke what he needed to say and said it with power; he believed in what he said and greatly influenced the population around him. I felt his influence from here [Florida] all the way to Augusta, Georgia. C. K. stood in the face of violence; they could not scare him during the Tallahassee bus boycott in Tallahassee, Florida. He spoke truth to power.

Father Pinder was a man of passion and goodwill. Both white and black people respected him. He was a great soul to know, and he had great influence; I respected him highly. My civil rights days started in Georgia. We moved on to Augusta, Georgia, where I really was involved in being president of the Southern Christian Leadership Conference [SCLC], vice president, and then president of Operation Mountaintop. My church served as a headquarters for the SCLC. We participated in everything good for blacks. We participated in demonstrations all the way through Eastern Georgia, and I became a delegate, the first black delegate to the Democratic Party on the Jimmy Carter ticket.

Researcher: Dr. Sims, what do you think the role of the black church is today?

Dr. Sims: I think that the black church at one time had greater strength in the male population. Now we don't have many males, and that is a disgrace. I see the black church today as being a women's movement, and that shouldn't be. You find that most black Baptist churches are packed with women, and black men are in some little corner of the church. Women are in leadership. I believe women should be in the church. The absence of a black male voice in the church has affected the church and shows up in the home. It is a terrible state, the black church has lost some of its power. And until we get the black man back and active in the church, it is not going to change. I think the young pastors fear the male population in church. I don't think we do enough to reach out to train the deacon. Reach out to train the laymen and use him so that they would want to come. After all,

> what is he going to do besides just sit there and do nothing? We have stopped the black man from having any power in the church. We stopped devotion and moved to praise service. The young black pastor is not involved in civil rights. On Sunday mornings, you do not hear many sermons that have the elements of civil rights in them, nor do you see many young black pastors taking a stand against injustice.[33]

Reflection on Interview 2: Rev. Dr. Arthur Sims Sr.

Dr. Sims's testimony reminds us that social justice preaching is not a recent phenomenon but an enduring practice that stretches across generations. His reference to the dual role of black pastors and morticians as mobilizers of the people is particularly striking, showing how deeply embedded clergy were—and are—in the social, spiritual, and political fabric of black life. He does not romanticize the past but offers a sober reflection on the current state of the black church, especially the absence of black men in the pews and pulpits.

This interview serves as a call to action. Dr. Sims's concern about the decline of male engagement in church life highlights a contemporary crisis of presence and participation. His critique challenges young pastors to reclaim the prophetic courage of predecessors like C. K. Steele. His words suggest that embodied preaching today must address external injustice and internal church dynamics that hinder inclusive leadership and communal empowerment. His life and ministry embody the enduring relevance of preaching that doesn't just inform but transforms.

Interview 3: Mrs. Marion Pinder

Mrs. Marion Grant Pinder is the wife of the late Father Nelson Pinder, who was born and raised in Jacksonville, Florida. Mrs. Pinder

33. From the author's interview of Dr. Sims.

is a Florida native and former educator of thirty years. She graduated from Bethune-Cookman University with a degree in social studies. During her matriculation at Bethune-Cookman, she met her husband of over sixty years—Father Nelson W. Pinder. Father Pinder received an opportunity to serve at the Episcopal Church of Saint John the Baptist in Orlando, Florida—where he ministered for over fifty years. Together, they raised two children—Gail Pinder and Nelson W. Pinder II. Marian was instrumental in Father Pinder's civil rights work in Orlando as she was very active in various initiatives from Sunday school to the altar guild as first lady of Saint John the Baptist Episcopal Church. She is a member of Alpha Kappa Alpha Sorority and an emeritus member of the Orlando chapter of The Girl Friends.

> *Researcher*: Mrs. Pinder, did you grow up Episcopal, and were the churches mixed?
>
> *Mrs. Pinder*: Yes, I grew up Episcopal. Back in the 1950s and 1960s, the churches were not mixed. They were predominantly black Episcopal churches; they were nice-sized churches. We had three hundred or more members, a nice choir, and a full-time priest. My mother was Episcopalian but most of my family was Baptist. So, it was very unusual for me to meet Nelson, who was studying to be an Episcopal priest at Bethune Cookman College.
>
> *Researcher*: Mrs. Pinder, what impact did Father Pinder have in Orlando during the Civil Rights Movement?
>
> *Mrs. Pinder*: Nelson was on the frontlines integrating a lot of places in the city of Orlando. He was involved with sit-ins at Woolworths and the five-and-dime store on Orange Avenue. He took a group of kids or teenagers to participate in social engagements, and they did sit-ins. He was one of the first members of the mayor's biracial committee to look into integrating different institutions in the city. He was the first that was over the Head Start program that came to Orlando. He helped a lot with integrating the public schools in Orlando. He was a first in a lot of things, and he was fearless. He had a

loud vocal voice that when he talked, you could not help but hear him. He was not afraid to meet with the white people across the city, and they learned to respect him in the end because he would not back down. It was just a hard fight and a long journey. But he was determined to change Orlando because the first time he told the story was when he flew into Orlando from Wisconsin. To interview for this job as parish priest. He was at the airport and he wanted to take a cab into the city, but the white cab wouldn't bring him into the city, they told him he couldn't ride in the white cab. He said, well, he just wanted a ride to Terry Street. He didn't care whether it was a white or black cab, but they refused to let him ride in the cab. Then he went to get a cup of coffee, and they refused. So, then he always tells the story that, "I have a lot of work to do in this city," so that's how it all started.

Researcher: Wow. I heard he was called "the whole priest," yet how did he get that name?

Mrs. Pinder: Because he would go into the alleys, back streets, anywhere, preaching the message of Jesus Christ and helping those who could not help themselves. Some considered him to be above people, but he would help everyone, and he would walk the streets. He would hang out at the Washington Shores Shopping Center, on Paramore Street, and anywhere that he thought he could help. Someone named him the "Hoodlum Priest" or the "Street Priest."

Researcher: Mrs. Pinder, how did Father Pinder influence the passing of civil rights legislation?

Mrs. Pinder: Well, they had this biracial committee; the mayor at the time was instrumental in influencing legislation. The best way to try to bring something good and some calmness to the city was to bring the people from both races together. So, they founded this advisory board called the Biracial Committee for Orlando, and then they discussed different issues and brought them before the city council. They did not always get what they wanted but kept working at it, and others who lived in the community joined the committee. For some reason, Orlando did not have riots like other cities. That was a big thing because the leaders worked hard at the table or demanded that the city give equal rights to the firefighters. The firefighters were not getting equal pay, so they negotiated with the police officers, and it was just a lot of negotiating. So, he had a pleasant working relationship with the city fathers, a very firm one, but he would not back down. He would talk up in a very loud and deep voice.

Researcher: Mrs. Pinder, did Father Pinder have any black pastors or preaching contemporaries while fighting for social justice in Orlando?

Mrs. Pinder: In Orlando, we had Reverend Judge, who has a street named for him. He was very active in the Civil Rights Movement. They had what is called a Black Ministerial Alliance, where they would meet to negotiate, strategize, and present to the city fathers. They worked it as much as possible and would have protest marches. However, they didn't carry any violence and followed Martin Luther King's idea of nonviolence. But we still had some brutality with the police, and then they would go straight to the chief of police and discuss it.

Researcher: Mrs. Pinder, do you think there was a risk of preaching on social justice issues from the pulpit then and now?

Mrs. Pinder: Nelson always preached about social justice issues from the pulpit on Sundays. It was not always easy for him [Father Pinder] because the Episcopal Church is predominately a white church, to speak. During his time, he did have quite a bit of white Episcopalians saying things about Nelson, who went to the bishop complaining about him saying things in the community. It just so happened we had a liberal bishop who was white. Bishop Falwell was his name and supported Nelson in any way. Bishop Falwell would tell the white Episcopalian who felt that [Father Pinder] was not supporting their church, "As long as he [Father Pinder] was not doing anything immoral or committing an immoral act, he is free to do whatever he needed to do for justice." It was not easy, and it was not an easy road. People would call the house sometimes and say derogatory things. You would be denied access to certain places, but you just had to keep pushing. Nelson was determined to make Orlando a different place and to make it great.

Researcher: Mrs. Pinder, how important was black sacred music during the Civil Rights Movement?

Mrs. Pinder: Black sacred music, the songs were very important, and the songs always told a story. You know, gospel music is our music, and they sang it at all their rallies. We loved it. We loved gospel music. He loved gospel music. They would have concerts, you know, they would bring the Bethune-Cookman choir over sometimes for a fundraiser to help with the cost, and they would be outstanding. Then, all of our churches around here usually had really good choirs, and we had Mount Pleasant Baptist Church, Shiloh Baptist Church, and Mount Zion Institutional Baptist Church. The ministers would have Emancipation Sunday which was around New Year's. They would go from church to church and have big rallies, you know, have gospel singing, and they would bring an outstanding Baptist preacher; most of the speakers were Baptist preachers. They would bring the crowd, and they would take up a collection, and that collection would help with the Ministerial Alliance project. So, music was very important. I think music will always be a part of the black culture.

Researcher: Mrs. Pinder, what significance did Florida have during slavery and the Civil Rights Movement?

Mrs. Pinder: Florida holds a lot of significance. They used to have big rallies in St. Augustine back in the day, back in the 1960s. I think Dr. King even came to St. Augustine, and they would rally and march. They had a lot of marches, and there was a lot going on, and you have to give it to the black ministers. Very few did not participate; most of them were out there marching. They

> were out there, and we have to appreciate that because the church was so important; it was such an important part of our lives during that time. I can't honestly say that now. But we need to go back. We need to get back to that because the kids, you know. They, the ones that are doing good now had good foundations from the church. It's part of our history, and I just appreciate all the black ministers. Some are stronger than others, but we need them all.
>
> My husband's monument is located on Parramore at Church Street and Terry Avenue, dedicated by the city of Orlando. He died prior to the city naming the street after him, but he knew it was coming. [34]

Reflection on Interview 3: Mrs. Marion Pinder

Mrs. Pinder's recollections about Father Nelson Pinder expand our understanding of the hidden costs and profound courage behind social justice ministry. She paints a portrait of a priest who walked the streets, challenged systemic oppression, and used his voice even when it risked institutional backlash. Her perspective adds critical depth to the narrative by showing the role of family, particularly clergy spouses, in supporting prophetic ministry.

Her account also emphasizes the importance of partnerships between black clergy and local government, as well as the strategic formation of biracial committees to preempt civil unrest. What stands out is her clear sense that music, memory, and movement were all tightly woven into the civil rights struggle. The story of Father Pinder's confrontation with racial discrimination the moment he arrived in Orlando underscores how embodied social justice preaching is forged in real-life encounters with injustice. Her interview reminds us that preaching must sound in the sanctuary and be seen in the streets.

34. From author's interview of Mrs. Pinder.

Interview 4: Rev. Dr. Larry G. Mills Sr.

Dr. Mills is the CEO of Mount Sinai Missionary Baptist Church in Orlando, is currently serving on the Orlando Utilities Commission (OUC) Board of Commissioners, and is the first black OUC president. Originally from Detroit, he has more than three decades of ministry experience. In 2007, Dr. Mills retired after twenty-three years with Lockheed Martin, where he served as corporate vice president of both human resources and business conduct for corporate operations. In 2020, Dr. Mills retired after thirty-two years with Mount Sinai Missionary Baptist Church, where he served as CEO and pastor, but not from his calling of preaching and teaching the word of God. Dr. Mills attended Wayne State University, University of Phoenix, and Bethany Theological Seminary and holds degrees in business management, religious education, sacred theology, and organizational management.

Active in community affairs, Dr. Mills has served on numerous boards and worked with groups to address homelessness in central Florida. He oversees the Mount Sinai Missionary Baptist Church Free Food Pantry, which serves four hundred people each week. He is the former president of the African American Council on Christian Clergy and is a member of the Boy Scouts Executive Council, Central Florida Urban League, formerly the Metropolitan Orlando Urban League, the NAACP, and the Inter-Denominational Faith Council. In addition, he is an author, recipient of numerous awards for leadership and community service, and a proud lifelong member of Phi Beta Sigma Fraternity.

Dr. Mills is a renowned leader in our community. His business experience, community involvement, and widespread knowledge will benefit the community and country as he continues to preach and teach the word of God locally and abroad.

> *Researcher*: Dr. Mills, can you tell me your name and a little bit about your background?
>
> *Dr. Mills*: Yes, I recently retired after thirty-two years of pastoring the Mount Sinai Missionary Baptist Church, and prior to that, I retired seven years ago as a vice

president of human resources for Lockheed Martin Corporation. I have dual degrees in religion as well as in business. A bachelor of science in business management and a bachelor of arts in religious education. Master of arts in organizational development, a master of science in sacred theology, and a ThD, doctor of sacred ministry, as well. I have been involved in various community affairs and events and have chaired many different areas of community involvement. Currently, I serve as the chairman of the board of commissioners for the Orlando Utilities Commission. So, in saying all that in a nutshell. I have a good feel for business, a good feel for the community, and a good feel for the church.

Researcher: Dr. Mills, how have African American preachers influenced the Civil Rights Movement?

Dr. Mills: I think they galvanized it and, in some areas, launched it. I think a lot of the activity from the civil rights and social change originated through the black church and the collaboration of the black church. Eventually, electing liberal-minded and black politicians, and the first stop the politicians made was the church. And so, I believe the church was a forerunner in a lot and sustained a lot and created a safe haven, if you will, for people to speak out through the church and not be victimized or feel retaliation as severe. So, I think they had a very prominent role, and if I may just say it, and I don't see that role as powerful as I did back then. The church of today, I believe, has split so into denominations, factions, and congregations that we have become almost isolated in our denominations in our own walls and confines. You don't have that unilateral reach across, and you don't—for example, at one point, I was president of the African American Council of Christian Clergy. okay, and a lot of your black elected officials in Orlando and Orange County, like Mayor Jerry Demings, Val Demings, Regina Hill back in the day, it was Maple Butler, okay. They were strong influences and collaborers [read: collaborators] with the pastors of that era. The F. L. Maxwells, the J. W. Toomers, the Hardgrits—these were the men who helped elect those politicians and worked across denominational lines and other affiliations to bring people together and provide leadership. When I was president of the African American Council, every person I've just named came to that meeting before launching anything. They sought our approval and wanted to run their plans by us to hear what we thought would happen. I don't feel that or see that as much. I see individuals trying to do their thing, but I don't see that cohesiveness and that solidarity among the black preachers and denominations, you know. And let me give you an example when you look from the fraternal and sorority standpoint. When you want to do something in the Greek, through black fraternities and sororities, everyone, whether they've gone to college or not, everyone has heard of the Divine Nine. And that Panhellenic council is the most powerful; none of the Divine Nine is going to venture out without a nod from the Panhellenic council. Okay, and so you see a solidarity even though they're different, and fraternity, sorority, we don't have that overarching unification anymore that had the power in the past, and that's where we are hurting.

Researcher: Dr. Mills, do you think there was a risk of preaching on social justice from the pulpit then and now?

Dr. Mills: Oh, yeah. The risk now and then was if you alienated the wrong political organization or person. Oh, oftentimes, your 501(c)(3) they would examine and try to find ways to strip it. Access to grants and funding was sometimes limited and impacted by your activity. Sad to say, oftentimes, within the black community itself, you were alienated, and people ostracized you. What does that have to do with God? Et cetera. So, you put yourself out there, and pretty much in religious jargon, you left yourself in the hands of God to be your protection. And so, yeah, it took courage to want to step out and to do that. And some were hurt, and some rose to prominence, but even those who rose to prominence suffered hardships as a result.

Researcher: Dr. Mills, what are your thoughts on the reemergence of racism in America?

Dr. Mills: I salute Donald Trump, and when I say that this is what I mean: I salute Donald Trump for bringing racism out of the closet. Donald Trump is so flamboyant and cocky that he gives DeSantis room to eliminate black history, to eliminate diversity positions in colleges. They removed funding if you bring up EEO officer or diversity. They are attacking all of that, and you see more and more KKK emblems and Confederate flags. Trump, in his era as president, kind of "undercoverly" released it. And so, people are becoming . . . And where racism was buried and those who had it, you know, were in the closet, it's now spreading, and you'll see that more and more so if we're not careful, it will bleed back into hiring practices and education.

Researcher: Dr. Mills, what do you think the role of the black church is today?

Dr. Mills: I see the church is more focused—and don't get this wrong. The church is more focused on individual salvation than global community concern. The church should always be about salvation, should always be about getting men into heaven. But there is a key Scripture that we have ignored. Matthew 25:36: "I was hungry and you fed me. I was naked and you clothed me." Matthew 25:40: "For as often as you do it to the least of one of those." That's mission, and to do mission, "Go ye, therefore." You got to go. And if you go, you're going to get exposed to social disorder and political segregation and other things, and then that's when you begin to be global-minded. And so until the church really gets back, into not the mission in Africa but a mission around the corner, okay, and only then will we regain our social prominence and be change agents. I would just like to say, what you're looking into is very needed, and if we're not careful, you know, if we go to sleep in the era in which we live, we can set up a world where all of our progress is lost for our children. We have to get our children rooted and grounded and focused in the area of social- and mission-mindedness to make it. That's it. [35]

35. From the author's interview of Dr. Mills.

Reflection on Interview 4: Rev. Dr. Larry G. Mills Sr.

Dr. Larry Mills offers both a historical perspective and a contemporary critique. His dual expertise in corporate leadership and pastoral ministry allows him to speak authoritatively about the institutional fragmentation of today's black church. Mills echoes the concern of scholars like Evelyn Brooks Higginbotham, PhD, the Victor S. Thomas, professor of history and African and African American studies at Harvard University, who warned of the dangers of losing institutional solidarity among black churches.[36] His lament over the decline of cross-denominational collaboration highlights the necessity of recovering a united prophetic front in the face of reemergent racism.

Mills's analogy to the Divine Nine's cohesive structure is a compelling challenge to pastors to rethink their ecclesial affiliations and communal responsibilities. His reflections on Trump-era racism, DeSantis's policies, and the erosion of DEI efforts demand a bold preaching that calls systems to account. He says, "Preaching that is not mission-minded will fail to fulfill the gospel imperative of Matthew 25."[37] For Mills, embodied social justice preaching must re-center the church as a moral compass, cultural refuge, and public conscience.

36. Higginbotham, *Righteous Discontent*, 221.

37. From the author's interview of Dr. Mills.

CHAPTER FIVE

CONCLUSION

THIS BOOK SERVES AS a model for the church and African American preachers to learn how to address social justice issues in and through embodied preaching. I hope this study will be used in black churches to inform the development of strategies, theories, and practices that address social justice issues through African American preaching. Additionally, the book may contribute to broadening our understanding of the connection between religion and social justice in the African American community. I hope this book will be disseminated through Bible colleges, seminaries, and churches.

In the final analyses, there was a unanimous consensus among all the people whom I was privileged to interview that there still is a need for the black church, the black preacher, and black America to speak out against social injustice, discrimination, racism, and sexism, and to keep up the fight for equality. It is alarming to discover how many young black pastors and churches have become isolated and insulated with their own issues and lack the overall care and concern for the global church. Further study should be done on the state of the black church and this generation of black pastors and preachers who are not as strong and are not as concerned as the black community of clergy of yesteryear. Today's black pastors are smarter, but spiritually, they seem to be much weaker than the preachers of the Civil Rights Movement era.

Existential exegesis is focused on the embodied experiences and the individual inner consent and fulfillment of the black pastor's purpose or calling in life. Black preachers and missional pastors must do an existential exegesis on themselves based on their feelings, convictions, interests, circumstances, and concerns. Jemar Tisby maintains,

> The struggle for human dignity is a spiritual and theological pursuit. The phrases "I am a man," "Black is beautiful," and "Black lives matter" are theological statements. They all express the biblical concept of the "image of God" and serve as affirmations of the inherent dignity and worth of Black people in an anti-Black world.[1]

No one wants freedom more than those who have been denied it. Black Americans have seen the worst of this country, yet our faith in God allows us to hope for the best.

I conclude this book with a scriptural reference from Luke the physician, found in Luke 23:34–35, and two historical references from the Reverend Dr. Martin Luther King Jr. and the German pastor Martin Niemöller.

> [But Jesus said, "Father, forgive them, for they don't know what they are doing."] Then they threw dice to divide his clothes. The people also stood there watching, but the leaders ridiculed him, saying, "He saved others. Let him save himself if he is the Christ of God, his chosen one! (Luke 23:34–35 NET; brackets original)

In this passage, Jesus asked his Father to forgive them. We often forget that it was the religious elite, the privileged, equivalent to our "church folk," that Jesus was praying for. These believers in God, believers in Yahweh, Elohim, were the reason Jesus was crucified on that Friday afternoon. It was the church folk, the scribes, the Pharisees, and the chief priests, who conspired to kill him. It was the church folk that Luke called the leaders who wanted to

1. Tisby (@JemarTisby), "The struggle for human dignity is a spiritual and theological pursuit," Twitter, Mar. 20, 2024, 7:08 p.m., https://x.com/JemarTisby/status/1770588260311375948.

shut Jesus down. John, the beloved disciple, tells us in John 11 that the chief priests and the Pharisees called a meeting of the Sanhedrin (church folk). Moreover, the church folk said, "If we let Jesus go on like this, everyone will believe in him, and then the Romans will come and take away both our temple and our nation" (John 11:48, NET). Church folk cared more about the rotten Roman government in power than they did about the righteous and reigning God in heaven, so they plotted to take his life.

The church folk were the reason Jesus was crucified, and I want to suggest that Jesus was saying it was the church folk who did not know what they were doing. The leaders of the church stirred up the crowds, lying on Jesus and hating on Jesus. They did not know what they were doing; the leaders of the church, throughout his ministry, were dogging Jesus, debating him about silly things like diets, which day of the week was sacred, and whose wife, a remarried widow, would be when she got to heaven? They debated Jesus about selling things while their people were being crushed by the occupying Roman government and crushed by cruel and crooked "church" requirements and preoccupation with tithing while overlooking justice.

"The average poor Palestinian farmer paid as much as 40 percent of his annual income to the Roman government and the local Jewish lackeys who were put in office by the Romans."[2] The temple tax was required by the priests at the church house. Leaders of the church debated Jesus about doctrine and dogma while members of the church were suffering under political and ecclesiastical oppression. The leaders of the church did not know what they were doing. Jesus called them blind guides straining at a gnat and swallowing a camel (see Matt 23:24 KJV). Here, they are putting to death the very one who came to give them life. I suggest that Jesus asks God to forgive the church folk because they do not know what they are doing. Luke 23:35 (NRSV) tells us, "And the people stood by," silently watching.

Historically, Dr. King said these words over fifty years ago, and yet they still ring true today. The church, the universal church,

2. Horsley, *Jesus and the Spiral*, 72–74.

must say something when they see injustice and wrongdoing. King said, "History will have to record that the greatest tragedy of this period of social transition was not the strident clamor of the bad people, but the appalling silence of the good people."[3] History should record that the greatest tragedy of the Civil Rights Movement was not the strident clamor or the loud protest or opposition of the bad people, all the name-calling that the bad people did all the time, but the silence of those who didn't say anything.

I have been on my own journey of constructivism—the process of piecing together knowledge that includes lived experience. My elders in Gary, Indiana, where I was born, suffered deeply. My grandparents and parents moved to Gary during the Great Migration from the South in search of better lives and employment opportunities. Instead, they were demeaned and degraded. Epithets of condescension were hurled at them as if such language were ordinary. They were called "nigger," "gal," "uncle," and "boy"—the same dehumanizing slurs routinely shouted at thousands of nonviolent, peaceful protesters during the Civil Rights Movement.

They had to get off the sidewalk when white people passed by. Every drinking fountain, every back door, every courtroom, every hospital, every act of legislation, every police authority said to them, "You do not matter."

My forefathers and mothers were made to feel like nothing all week long. They were maids, cooks, chauffeurs, domestics, and gardeners. Monday through Saturday, they were nothing and nobody. But a strange dignity caught them on Sunday morning. A sense of grandeur overwhelmed them, and I heard them singing, "Over my head, I hear music in the air. There must be a God somewhere." They were pastors, preachers, deacons, and missionaries on Sunday. They had some sense of power, position, and prestige in the black church.

The strident clamor, shouting from police cars. The strident clamor yelled while fire hoses knocked down women, children, and young people who were only asking for equality under the law, who were asking for an equal right to vote, equal opportunity,

3. King, *Stride Toward Freedom*, 202.

quality education, and equal access to healthcare. The greatest tragedy was not the negative noise and name-calling of the bad people. The greatest tragedy, according to Dr. King, was not the strident clamor of the bad people. The greatest tragedy was the appalling silence of the good people. Jesus said, "Father, forgive them, for they do not know what their silence is doing. They do not know what their silence is saying." Yet, their silence speaks volumes. Back in the Civil Rights Movement, the silence of the church spoke volumes. In the contemporary Black Lives Matter movement, the silence of the church still speaks volumes.

Return to the silence I referenced earlier—specifically that of prominent mainstream black pastors like Dr. Tony Evans, Bishop T. D. Jakes, and Voddie Baucham. Their notable absence in the public discourse around racial injustice, systemic inequality, and social transformation is deafening. These men have massive platforms and influence yet often lean toward safer subjects like prosperity, individual sanctification, or personal responsibility. Could this be a strategic silence? Is it possible that their ministries, undergirded in part by white evangelical financial support, have led them to choose preservation of their platforms over prophetic truth-telling?

Barbara Brown Taylor's conviction rings loud: "The only clear line I draw these days is this: when my religion tries to come between me and my neighbor, I will choose my neighbor. . . . Jesus never commanded me to love my religion."[4] The prophetic witness demands a courageous love for neighbor—even when it costs something. And perhaps that's the problem. There may be a fine line between wise discretion and fearful avoidance. But we must ask, Who benefits when the church is quiet in the face of injustice? Who suffers? In this age of cancel culture, where one wrong word can dismantle a ministry or destroy a reputation, many choose silence. But prophetic ministry was never meant to be safe. The witness of Jesus and the prophets is not one of safety but of sacrifice.

Above, I mentioned the black historical reference from Dr. King. Now I turn to a white European historical reference from

4. Taylor, *Holy Envy*, 208.

Niemöller, the German pastor, who put it this way some seventy years ago, in 1946. When the Nazis were in power in Germany, Niemöller talked about the danger of silence and not speaking up. "Pastor Martin Niemöller is best known for writing First They Came—one of the most famous poems about the Holocaust."[5]

> First they came for the Communists
> And I did not speak out
> Because I was not a Communist
> Then they came for the Socialists
> And I did not speak out
> Because I was not a Socialist
> Then they came for the trade unionists
> And I did not speak out
> Because I was not a trade unionist
> Then they came for the Jews
> And I did not speak out
> Because I was not a Jew
> Then they came for me
> And there was no one left
> To speak out for me.[6]

The greatest tragedy in Nazi Germany was not the nasty names spat out by the Nazis, the bad people. The greatest tragedy was the failure of the good people to speak out against the horrible Holocaust of the Jewish people. In the words of Luke, "And the people stood by watching" (Luke 23:35 NRSV). The people stood by, silently watching. They did not say a word. They did not speak up against law enforcement. Roman soldiers were murdering an innocent man, and their response was silence. An unarmed black man was being senselessly, brutally slain, and the church was silent.

The greatest tragedy, from the death of Emmett Till through to the death of Medgar Evers, to the murder of Schwerner, Goodman, and Chaney in Philadelphia, Mississippi, to the murder of Dr. King himself in Memphis, Tennessee, the greatest tragedy, from the lynchings of the Ku Klux Klan in the 1800s and through

5. Holocaust Memorial Day Trust, "Pastor Martin Niemöller."

6. Niemöller, "First They Came."

the first half of the 1900s to the terrorist slaughter of the "Charleston 9" at Emanuel African Methodist Episcopal Church in 2015 at a Bible study, the greatest tragedy is not the nasty noises coming from the mouths of the bad people. The greatest tragedy is the appalling silence of the good people. The church's silence has been deafening. Father, forgive them; however, they do not know what their silence is doing. They do not know what their silence is saying. Their silence speaks loudly. The church must realize that silence is our weakness, and sound is our weapon.

The reason why young people are so messed up today is that we are not telling them our stories. We are not reminding them of how far God has brought us, how many doors God has opened for us, how many ways God has made for us, and how many prayers God has answered for us. Even though Governor DeSantis is trying to water down our history, the black preacher must continue to be the leader in the church, community, and social engagements. The fight for freedom, equity, and inclusion must continue today. In my final analysis, this book concludes that social injustice and inequality that habitually delay human thriving and the common good have been pursued by many preachers who stood for social justice in Florida, and social injustice must continue to be overcome by the love of Christ demonstrated through embodied sermons.

In conclusion, Governor Ron DeSantis represents one of the most visible and alarming examples of contemporary efforts to marginalize black people through policy and education. His administration has taken deliberate steps to erase or distort African American history in Florida's public schools. Through legislation like the "Stop W.O.K.E. Act," DeSantis has banned the honest teaching of systemic racism and historical truths. He has restructured curricula to emphasize so-called "positive contributions" of enslaved people, suggesting that they benefited from slavery. Furthermore, he rejected the College Board's AP African American studies course, calling it "historically inaccurate" and politically driven.[7] These actions amount to a whitewashing of America's racial past and a strategic suppression of truth.

The black pulpit has historically been a prophetic voice against oppression. In the face of such modern-day erasure, black preaching must reclaim that role with boldness. Just as the Old Testament prophets spoke truth to power in unjust systems, today's preachers must name what is happening, expose its spiritual and social implications, and lead their congregations in resistance through truth-telling, education, and activism. The silence of prominent black preachers in the face of these injustices is a spiritual crisis. When our pulpits go quiet, injustice gains ground. We can no longer complain and comply as black preachers; we must act now!

RECOMMENDATIONS FOR CHURCHES

- *Preach with Prophetic Clarity*: Sermons should name the harm being done by political leaders like DeSantis and connect it to biblical mandates for justice and truth.
- *Educate the Congregation*: Churches should hold forums, Bible studies, and reading groups on the true history of black people in America and the dangers of revisionism.
- *Partner Across Racial Lines*: Black and white churches must come together to resist false narratives and support inclusive, honest curricula in local school boards and legislatures.
- *Advocate Publicly*: Churches should support educators, students, and parents resisting these changes and speak out at school board meetings, in op-eds, and through organized campaigns.
- *Center the Youth*: Equip young people with the tools to know their history and challenge misinformation. The church must affirm its identity in both Christ and culture.

DeSantis's policies are not just about education but power, identity, and control. And if the church remains silent, we betray

7. Contorno, "African American Studies Course."

our calling. Now is the time for black preaching to rise again with a double portion of conviction—telling the truth, preserving our story, and resisting the erasure of our dignity. Let the church be the keeper of our collective memory and the catalyst for prophetic action.

In a recent article from the American Civil Liberties Union (ACLU) titled "Anti-DEI Efforts Are the Latest Attack on Racial Equity and Free Speech" it reads, "Today, the extreme right's latest attack is aimed at dismantling diversity, equity, and inclusion (DEI) programs."[8] However, my research has concluded that while, sadly, many of our African American pastors, preachers, and leaders may have gone silent at a time when our nation needs their voice the most, many in the past and in more contemporary times have left a legacy on which we can stand as preachers engaged in pursuing social justice.

This book's research has shown that over the years, the black church, its missional pastors, and its preachers have become smarter but weaker in terms of social justice preaching. There is an individualistic spirit among the clergy and laity that lacks care and concern for the global or universal church. There seems to be a lack of black men participating in the worship service. In contrast, the role of black women has shifted and garnered them more power and responsibility within the modern black church community. There are internal and external risks in preaching social justice from the pulpit. From an internal standpoint, black pastors who preach on social issues and concerns will be confronted and challenged by their congregations. Prominent members of the black community of clergy may ostracize many pastors for standing up for social justice.

This research affirms that the urgency for social justice preaching within the black church is as critical today as it was during the Civil Rights Movement. However, there has been a marked shift in focus among many popular preachers—both black and white—toward messages centered on prosperity, individualism, and personal advancement, often at the expense of collective liberation

8. Watson, "Anti-DEI Efforts."

and justice. The prominence of figures such as Creflo Dollar and T. D. Jakes underscores a troubling trend: a widespread theological disengagement from the systemic issues that continue to plague African American communities. Their significant influence and vast platforms have too often substituted prophetic confrontation with spiritualized consumerism, comfort, and complacency.

The external risk would include government surveillance (i.e., Federal Bureau of Investigations), police harassment and brutality, political backlash, and the possibility that 501(c)(3) funding would be stripped away with no access to government grants. Last but certainly not least, missional pastors who preach on social justice could lose their lives. The need for social justice preaching today is the same or greater than it was during the height of the Civil Rights Movement. With Trump leading a reemergence of racism in America, black pastors must speak out against indifference, stigmas, biases, stereotypes, prejudices, and discrimination. This is not the time for the black church and the black pastor to develop compassion fatigue, but we must be resolute and continue to speak truth to power from the pulpit. The African American missional pastors must decide to show up with empathy—that is, to embody charity, grace, and the best of our virtues—in the continued fight for freedom, justice, and equality. More research should be done on this matter.

Appendix A

Primary Ethnographic Sources

Name	*Interview Dates*
Mr. Ernest P. Boyd	September 12, 2023
Rev. Dr. Eddie J. Williamson	February 20, 2024
Rev. Dr. Robert Spooney	February 23, 2024
Mrs. Marion Pinder	February 25, 2024
Ms. Crystal Priester	February 25, 2024
Rev. Dr. R. B. Holmes Jr.	February 29, 2024
Rev. Derek Steele	February 29, 2024
Rev. Dr. Johnny Turner	March 1, 2024
Rev. Dr. Arthur D. Sims Sr.	March 2, 2024
Rev. Dr. Larry G. Mills Sr.	March 4, 2024
Elder Frederick N. Owens	March 8, 2024

Appendix B

Informed Consent Form for Personal Interview

SOUTH FLORIDA THEOLOGICAL SEMINARY, DEERFIELD BEACH, FLORIDA

My name is ____________________, and I am collecting information as part of my doctoral program at South Florida Theological Seminary. My advisor is _________, and we would like to invite you to participate in the project described below. I will explain this document to you in detail. Please feel free to ask questions. If you have more questions later, I will be happy to discuss them with you at any time.

Description of the project:

- You are being invited to participate in the study because _________________.
- As a participant you will be invited to volunteer your time for this research study.
- The interview will take approximately_______________(minutes/hours) to complete.

- This research will help to clarify ______________________ ______________________, and this information will contribute to Christian ministry by ____________________________ __________..You will be one of about ______ participants who will be interviewed individually.

Procedures:

I will have questions prepared for you to answer about ____________________.

Details (student: delete or adapt the points below to suit your own needs):

- ·We will meet at a convenient location for you. It may be your home if you prefer.
- ·I will ask you to answer the questions while my audio recording device is on. Recording your answers will help me to take home accurate information from the interview. The recording will be written up on a document on my computer later.
- ·My assistant will be present with us as someone who can assist us in our interview process in any way you may need.
- ·If necessary, a translator will also be present to help us.
- ·We will only meet once. It is possible that I will ask for a second meeting at a later time if I feel it would be helpful. Also, you may ask for a second visit in order to spend time together listening to the audio recording or to read through a printed manuscript of the interview. At that time you may share any concerns you might have about using your interview for research.

Risks or discomfort: (Student: adapt for your own needs.)

My assistant and I will do our best to provide a private, safe, and comfortable place for the interview. Should you rather meet in your home, we recommend a private location, such as a home office. If for any reason the topic becomes emotionally uncomfortable for you, or if for any other reason you become uncomfortable, you may ask to stop the interview. You may also ask that any portion be omitted from the final written manuscript.

Benefits of this study:

Volunteering for this study will have no direct benefit to you, but it will contribute greatly to understanding ____________. Through the information from your interview, people will learn about ________________________. If you would like a copy of the finished project, I will be happy to send that to you.

Confidentiality:

Your part in this study is confidential. (Student: adapt this to meet your own needs.)

None of the information reported will identify you by name, unless you choose to allow your name to appear in print. Please note that the consent forms will be stored ________________. The transcript of the interview will be stored in a separate place. It will be in my computer database, accessible only by my password. The transcript will be coded by a number and your name deleted.

Voluntary participation and withdrawal:

Participation in research is voluntary. You have the right to refuse to be in this study. If you decide to be in the study and change your mind, you have the right to drop out at any time. You may skip questions or refuse to answer a question whenever you like.

Questions, rights, and complaints:

If you have any questions about this research project, please call me, ________________, at this phone number ____________ or email me at ________________. If you have any questions or concerns about your rights as a research participant in this study, please direct them to Daphney Lundi at dlundi@sfbc.edu or Anna Droll at adroll@sfbc.edu.

Consent statement:

This statement certifies the following: that you are 18 years of age or older, and you have read the consent, and all your questions have been answered. If you are giving consent for your children or another dependent to participate, your signature certifies your consent. You understand that you (or the participant) may withdraw from the study at any time. All of the answers you provide will be kept private, unless you choose to allow your name to appear in print. Also, you have the right to see the results prior to their being published.

I consent to being a participant in this project being guided by Mr./Ms.________________________.

I check here that I may be contacted for any follow up questions. ____

I check here that I allow my name to appear in print. ____

________________________________ ____________________

Signature of Participant *Date*
or Legal Guardian or Representative

Appendix C

Research Questionnaire

Some of the questions posed to guide the gathering of historical data are featured below:

1. What impact did preachers have before the Civil Rights Movement?
2. How have African American preachers influenced social movements like the Civil Rights Movement? How has preaching influenced the passing of legislation on social justice?

Some of the questions dealing with preaching in Florida are featured below:

1. How did Father Pinder and Reverend Steele make an impact in Florida through their preaching?
2. Are social justice issues important to African American preachers in Florida today? Why or why not?
3. However, is the risk of preaching on social justice issues perceived too great in our contemporary context?
4. Tell me about the culture and climate in Orlando during the Civil Rights Movement.
5. What was a typical Sunday like for you growing up?

6. How important was black sacred music to the Civil Rights Movement?
7. What are your thoughts on the reemergence of racism in America?
8. What do you think the role of the black church is today?

Bibliography

ACLU Florida. "Remembering Ocoee." Last updated Nov. 1, 2022. https://www.aclufl.org/campaigns-initiatives/remembering-ocoee/.

African American Registry. "The Black Church in America, a Story." https://aaregistry.org/story/the-black-church-a-brief-history/.

African Methodist Episcopal. "Our History." https://www.ame-church.com/our-church/our-history/.

Alcántara, Jared E., ed. *Let the Legends Preach: Sermons by the Living Legends at the E. K. Bailey Preaching Conference*. Eugene, OR: Wipf & Stock, 2021.

Alexander, Estrelda. *Black Fire: One Hundred Years of African American Pentecostalism*. Downers Grove, IL: InterVarsity, 2011.

Allyn, Nelson. "Nat Turner's Rebellion, 1831." Gilder Lehrman Institute of American History. https://www.gilderlehrman.org/history-resources/spotlight-primary-source/nat-turner%E2%80%99s-rebellion-1831.

Anderson, Carol Elaine. *White Rage: The Unspoken Truth of Our Racial Divide*. New York: Bloomsbury, 2016.

Angell, Stephen Ward. "Henry McNeal Turner." New Georgia Encyclopedia, last updated Aug. 14, 2020. https://www.georgiaencyclopedia.org/articles/arts-culture/henry-mcneal-turner-1834–1915/.

Apostolic Archives International. "The Azusa Street Revival." https://www.apostolicarchives.com/articles/article/8801925/173190.htm.

Archives of the Episcopal Church. "The Reverend Absalom Jones, 1746–1818." The Church Awakens: African Americans and the Struggle for Justice. https://web.archive.org/web/20250424100935/https://episcopalarchives.org/church-awakens/exhibits/show/leadership/clergy/jones.

Austin, Beth. *1619: Virginia's First Africans*. Hampton History Museum, 2018. Revised 2019. https://www.hampton.gov/DocumentCenter/View/24075/1619-Virginias-First-Africans?bidId=.

Banks, Adelle M. "Q&A: From Ferguson to Baltimore, Black America's Faith Is Tested." RNS, May 1, 2015. https://religionnews.com/2015/05/01/qa-ferguson-baltimore-black-americas-faith-tested/.

Baucham, Voddie T. *Fault Lines: The Social Justice Movement and Evangelicalism's Looming Catastrophe*. Washington, DC: Salem, 2021.

Beatty, Robert. "South Florida Says Goodbye to Rev. Dr. Mack King Carter." *South Florida Times*, Oct. 10, 2013. http://www.sfltimes.com/uncategorized/south-florida-says-goodbye-to-rev-dr-mack-king-carter.

Bethel Missionary Baptist Church. "Rev. Dr. R. B. Holmes, Jr., Pastor." https://betheltally.org/about/dr-r-b-holmes.

Blackburn, Robin. *The Making of New World Slavery: From the Baroque to the Modern, 1492–1800*. New York: Verso, 1997.

Blount, Brian K. *Then the Whisper Put on Flesh: New Testament Ethics in an African American Context*. Nashville: Abingdon, 2001.

Bonhoeffer, Dietrich. *The Cost of Discipleship*. With a foreword by Eric Metaxas. With a "Memoir" by Gerhard Leibholz. New York: Touchstone, 2018.

Brau, Bekki. "Constructivism." In *The Students' Guide to Learning Design and Research*, edited by Royce Kimmons and Secil Caskurlu. 2020. https://edtechbooks.org/studentguide/constructivism.

Brown, Alaijah. "Rev. R. B. Holmes' Task Force Symposium: Crafting New Black History Curriculum." *Tallahassee Democrat*, Feb. 25, 2024. https://www.tallahassee.com/story/news/local/2024/02/25/rev-holmes-hosts-conference-proposes-new-black-history-curriculum-bethel-baptist/72697336007/.

Byrnes, Joe. "Episcopal Priest and Civil Rights Leader Nelson Pinder Dies, Leaving a Profound Effect on His Church and Orlando." Central Florida Public Media, July 12, 2022. https://www.wmfe.org/2022–7–12/episcopal-priest-and-civil-rights-leader-nelson-pinder-dies-leaving-profound-effect-on-his-church-and-orlando.

Capital Outlook. "The 'Teaching Our Own History Task Force' Poised to Write Its Own Story." Sept. 19, 2023. https://capitaloutlook.com/the-teaching-our-own-history-task-force-poised-to-write-its-own-story/.

Chalmers, Aaron. *Interpreting the Prophets: Reading, Understanding, and Preaching from the Worlds of the Prophets*. Downers Grove, IL: InterVarsity, 2015.

The Church for the Fellowship of All Peoples. "About Us." https://www.fellowshipsf.org/.

The Circle Association. "The Niagara Movement." Buffalo.edu. http://www.math.buffalo.edu/~sww/ohistory/hwny-niagara-movement.html.

Clark, Edgar, III. "Hidden in Plain Sight: Reclaiming the Witness and Wisdom of Black Contemplative Preachers." *Homiletic* 47 (2022) 3–14. https://homiletic.net/index.php/homiletic/article/view/5367.

CME Church. "The Christian Methodist Episcopal Church." https://thecmechurch.org/about-us/.

COGIC. "Our Founder." https://www.cogic.org/about-us/our-founder/.

College Sidekick. "Life as a Slave in the Cotton Kingdom." African American History and Culture. https://www.collegesidekick.com/study-guides/atd-fscj-africanamericanhistory/life-as-a-slave-in-the-cotton-kingdom.

Collier-Thomas, Bettye. *Daughters of Thunder: Black Women Preachers and Their Sermons, 1850–1979*. San Francisco: Jossey-Bass, 1998.

Cone, James H. *Black Theology and Black Power: 50th Anniversary Edition.* Maryknoll, NY: Orbis, 2018.

———. *A Black Theology of Liberation: 50th Anniversary Edition.* Maryknoll, NY: Orbis, 2020. Kindle.

———. *God of the Oppressed.* Maryknoll, NY: Orbis, 2018.

———. *The Spirituals and the Blues: An Interpretation.* Maryknoll, NY: Orbis, 1991.

The Conference of National Black Churches (CNBC). "About the Conference of National Black Churches." https://www.thecnbc.net/about.

Contorno, Steve. "Florida Says Rejected AP African American Studies Course 'Lacks Educational Value.'" ABC7 News, Jan. 21, 2023. https://abc7news.com/post/florida-ap-african-american-studies-ron-desantis-what-is/12724464/?utm_source=chatgpt.com&userab=abcn_du_cat_topic_feature_holdout-474*variant_b_redesign-1939%2Cotv_web_content_rec-445*variant_c_trending-1851.

Croft, Wayne E., Sr. *The Motif of Hope in African American Preaching During Slavery and the Post–Civil War Era: There Is a Bright Side Somewhere (Rhetoric, Race, and Religion).* Lanham, MD: Lexington, 2017.

Crump, Benjamin L. *Open Season: Legalized Genocide of Colored People.* New York: Harper Collins, 2019. Kindle.

Dawson, Shay. "Harriet Tubman (1822–1913)." National Women's History Museum, 2024. https://www.womenshistory.org/education-resources/biographies/harriet-tubman.

Deagan, Kathleen A., and Jane Landers. "Fort Mose: Earliest Free African-American Town in the United States." In *I Too, Am America: Archaeological Studies of African-American Life,* edited by Theresa A. Singleton, 261–82. Charlottesville: University of Virginia Press, 1999. https://www.latinamericanstudies.org/slavery/Fort-Mose.pdf.

Detroit Historical Society. "Franklin, Clarence LaVaughn." https://detroithistorical.org/learn/encyclopedia-of-detroit/franklin-clarence-lavaughn.

Dickerson, Dennis C. "Our History." African Methodist Episcopal Church. https://www.ame-church.com/our-church/our-history/.

Douglass, Frederick. *Life and Times of Frederick Douglass.* Boston: De Wolfe, Fiske & Co. 1882.

Electronic Oberlin Group. "The Niagara Movement." Oberlin Through History. https://www2.oberlin.edu/external/EOG/Niagara%20Movement/niagaramain.htm.

Emory University News Center. "Anderson Explores Country's Racial Past, Present in 'White Rage.'" May 31, 2016. https://news.emory.edu/stories/2016/05/upress_white_rage_anderson/index.html.

Equal Justice Initiative. "Lynching in America: Confronting the Legacy of Racial Terror." 2017. https://eji.org/reports/lynching-in-america/.

Erickson, Millard J. *Christian Theology.* 3rd ed. Grand Rapids: Baker Academic, 2013.

Evans, Michael. *Leadership in the Black Church: Guidance in the Midst of Changing Demographics.* Fort Worth, TX: Austin Brothers, 2018. Kindle.

Felder, Cain Hope, ed. *Stony the Road We Trod: African American Biblical Interpretation.* Minneapolis: Fortress, 1991.

FEMA. *Engagement Guidelines: Black Church Protestant Leaders.* Department of Homeland Security, Tip Sheets: Engaging Faith Communities. https://www.fema.gov/sites/default/files/2020-3/fema_faith-communities_black-church-protestant-leaders_1.pdf.

Frazier, Franklin E. *The Negro Church in America.* New York: Schocken. 1964.

Full Gospel Baptist. "Leadership: Translating Vision into Reality." https://www.fullgospelbaptist.org/leadership/.

Gabi-Williams, Olatoun. Review of *The Underground Railroad* by Colson Whitehead. Borders, 2018. https://bordersliteratureonline.net/books/The-Underground-Railroad.

Gates, Henry Louis. *America Behind the Color Line: Dialogues with African Americans.* New York: Warner, 2004.

Gibson, Dawn-Marie. *A History of the Nation of Islam: Race, Islam, and the Quest for Freedom.* Santa Barbara, CA: Bloomsbury, 2012.

Gilbert, Kenyatta R. *Exodus Preaching: Crafting Sermons About Justice and Hope.* Nashville: Abingdon, 2018.

———. *A Pursued Justice: Black Preaching from the Great Migration to Civil Rights.* Waco, TX: Baylor University Press, 2017.

Golden, Marita. *Migrations of the Heart.* New York: Anchor, 1983.

Goñi-Lessan, Ana. "Faith Leaders, Educators Ask Florida Officials to Reconsider Black History Standards." *Tallahassee Democrat*, Feb. 27, 2024. https://www.tallahassee.com/story/news/politics/2024/02/27/florida-pastors-educators-give-state-education-officials-food-for-thought-on-black-history/72762046007/?itm_medium=recirc&itm_source=taboola&itm_campaign=internal&itm_content=SectionFrontFeed-FeedRedesign.

GreatHearts Institute. "Cornel West on the Moral Obligations of Living in a Democratic Society." Feb. 11, 2013. https://whatsoproudlywehail.org/cornel-west-on-the-moral-obligations-of-living-in-a-democratic-society.

Groody, Daniel G. *Globalization, Spirituality, and Justice: Navigating the Path to Peace.* Maryknoll, NY: Orbis, 2007. Kindle.

Hampton History Museum. "The 1619 Landing—Virginia's First Africans: Report and FAQs." https://hampton.gov/3580/The-1619-Landing-ReportFAQs.

Higginbotham, Evelyn Brooks. *Righteous Discontent: The Women's Movement in the Black Baptist Church, 1880–1920.* Cambridge: Harvard University Press, 1993.

Holocaust Memorial Day Trust. "Pastor Martin Niemöller." https://www.hmd.org.uk/resource/pastor-martin-niemoller-hmd-2021/.

Horsley, Richard A. *Jesus and the Spiral of Violence: Popular Jewish Resistance in Roman Palestine.* Minneapolis: Fortress, 1993.

Hubbard, Don. *The Sermon and the African American Literary Imagination.* Columbia, MO: University of Missouri Press, 1996.

Huff, Theresa. "Constructivism (Cognitive Constructivism)." Pressbooks. https://isu.pressbooks.pub/thuff/chapter/constructivism/.

Jeffres, Emily, and Natalie Sportelli. "Adam Clayton Powell Jr., Class of 1930." Colgate at 200 Years. https://200.colgate.edu/looking-back/people/adam-clayton-powell-jr-class-1930.

Jenkins, Philip. *The Next Christendom: The Coming of Global Christianity.* New York: Oxford University Press, 2011.

Jowett, Benjamin, trans. *The Dialogues of Plato.* 3rd ed. 1892. Lexundria. https://lexundria.com/plat_apol/38/j.

Keckley, Elizabeth. *Behind the Scenes: Or, Thirty Years a Slave and Four Years in the White House.* G.W. Carleton & Co., 1868. Kindle.

Keller, Timothy. *Generous Justice: How God's Grace Makes Us Just.* New York: Penguin, 2010.

King, Martin Luther, Jr. *Stride Toward Freedom: The Montgomery Story.* New York: Harper & Row, 1958.

Kostlevy, William. *Historical Dictionary of the Holiness Movement.* Lanham, MD: Scarecrow, 2009.

Landers, Jane G. *Black Society in Spanish Florida.* Urbana, IL: University of Illinois Press, 1999.

———. "Francisco Menéndez." Peoples of the Historical Slave Trade. https://enslaved.org/fullStory/16-23-92885/.

LaRue, Cleophus James. *The Heart of Black Preaching.* Louisville: Westminster John Knox, 2000.

———. *I Believe I Will Testify: The Art of African American Preaching.* Louisville: Westminster John Knox, 2011. Kindle.

———. *Power in the Pulpit: How America's Most Effective Black Preachers Prepare Their Sermons.* Louisville: Westminster John Knox, 2002.

———. *Rethinking Celebration: From Rhetoric to Praise in African American Preaching.* Louisville: Westminster John Knox, 2016.

LeFebvre, Michael L. "Neither Jew Nor Gentile: The Musings of a Modern Covenanter on Racial Reconciliation." *Reformed Presbyterian Theological Journal* 3 (2017) 32–42. https://journal.rpts.edu/2017/04/01/neither-jew-nor-gentile-the-musings-of-a-modern-covenanter-on-racial-reconciliation/.

Lincoln, C. Eric, and Lawrence H. Mamiya. *The Black Church in the African American Experience.* Durham, NC: Duke University Press, 1990.

Loewen, James W. *Sundown Towns: A Hidden Dimension of American Racism.* New York: New Press, 2005.

Marx, Karl, and Friedrich Engels. *The Communist Manifesto.* Minneapolis: Learner, 2017.

Mascolo, Michael F., and Kurt W. Fischer. "Constructivist Theories." In *The Cambridge Encyclopedia of Child Development,* edited by Brian Hopkins, 49–63. Cambridge: Cambridge University Press, 2005.

Massey, James Earl. *Stewards of the Story: The Task of Preaching.* Louisville: Westminster John Knox, 2006.

Mathews, Donald G. *Religion in the Old South*. Chicago: University of Chicago Press, 1977.

McCaulley, Esau. *Reading While Black: African American Biblical Interpretation as an Exercise in Hope*. Westmont, IL: IVP Academic, 2020.

McMickle, Marvin. *Where Have All the Prophets Gone?* Cleveland, OH: Pilgrim, 2006.

Michals, Debra, ed. "Mary McLeod Bethune (1875–1955)." National Women's History Museum, 2015. https://www.womenshistory.org/education-resources/biographies/mary-mcleod-bethune.

Mitchell, Henry H. *Black Church Beginnings: The Long-Hidden Realities of the First Years*. Grand Rapids: Eerdmans, 2004.

———. *Black Preaching: The Recovery of a Powerful Art*. Nashville: Abingdon, 1991. Kindle.

———. *Celebration and Experience in Preaching*. Nashville: Abingdon, 1990.

Momodu, Samuel. "The Ocoee Massacre (1920)." BlackPast, Oct. 31, 2020. https://www.blackpast.org/african-american-history/the-ocoee-massacre-1920/.

Moyd, Olin P. *The Sacred Art: Preaching and Theology in the African American Tradition*. Valley Forge, PA: Judson, 1995.

Murphy, Colleen. "What's the Difference Between Equity and Equality?" Health, last updated Apr. 13, 2024. https://www.health.com/mind-body/health-diversity-inclusion/equity-vs-equality.

NAACP. "NAACP Issues Travel Advisory in Florida." May 20, 2023. https://naacp.org/articles/naacp-issues-travel-advisory-florida.

National Archives. "13th Amendment to the U.S. Constitution: Abolition of Slavery (1865)." https://www.archives.gov/milestone-documents/13th-amendment.

Neely, Alan. "Liele, George (c. 1750–1828)." In *Biographical Dictionary of Christian* Missions, edited by Gerald H. Anderson. New York: Macmillan Reference USA, 1998. https://www.bu.edu/missiology/missionary-biography/l-m/liele-george-c-1750–1828/.

Newman, Richard S. *Freedom's Prophet: Bishop Richard Allen, the AME Church, and the Black Founding Fathers*. New York: New York University Press, 2008.

Niebuhr, Helmut Richard. *Christ and Culture*. New York: Harper & Bros., 1956.

Niemöller, Martin. "First They Came—By Pastor Martin Niemöller." Holocaust Memorial Day Trust. https://www.hmd.org.uk/resource/first-they-came-by-pastor-martin-niemoller/.

Orange County Regional History Center. "Yesterday, This Was Home: The Ocoee Massacre of 1920." https://www.thehistorycenter.org/exhibition/the-ocoee-massacre/.

Osgood, Rosalind V. "Our Founder." Mount Olive Development Corporation. https://www.modcocares.org/our-founder.

Oshatz, Molly. *Slavery and Sin: The Fight Against Slavery and the Rise of Liberal Protestantism*. New York: Oxford University Press, 2012.

Padgett, Gregory B. "C. K. Steele: A Biography." PhD diss., Florida State University, 1994.

Paulose, Paulose Mar. "Chapter 9: Religionless Christianity." In *Encounter in Humanization: Insights for Christian-Marxist Dialogue and Cooperation*. Prepared for Religion Online by Ted Brock and Winnie Brock. https://www.religion-online.org/book-chapter/chapter-9-religionless-christianity/.

PAW ECN West. "Our History." https://paw-ecnwest.org/our-history.

PBS. "Harriet Tubman." Africans in America. https://www.pbs.org/wgbh/aia/part4/4p1535.html.

Preaching.com. "Massey's 'The Burdensome Joy of Preaching' Named Year's Best." https://www.preaching.com/book-reviews/masseys-the-burdensome-joy-of-preaching-named-years-best/.

Raboteau, Albert J. *Slave Religion: The "Invisible Institution" in the Antebellum South*. New York: Oxford University Press, 1978.

Ratcliffe, Susan, ed. "Desmond Tutu 1931—South African Anglican Clergyman." In *Oxford Essential Quotations*. N.p.: Oxford University Press, 2017. https://www.oxfordreference.com/display/10.1093/acref/9780191843730.001.0001/q-oro-ed5–00016497.

Rothstein, Richard. *The Color of Law: A Forgotten History of How Our Government Segregated America*. New York: Liveright, 2017.

———. "'The Color of Law' Details How U.S. Housing Policies Created Segregation." Interview by Ari Shapiro, NPR, May 17, 2017. https://www.npr.org/2017/05/17/528822128/the-color-of-law-details-how-u-s-housing-policies-created-segregation.

Sanders, Cheryl J. *Saints in Exile: The Holiness-Pentecostal Experience in African American Religion and Culture*. New York: Oxford University Press, 1999.

Shenvi, Neil, and Pat Sawyer. *Critical Dilemma: The Rise of Critical Theories and Social Justice Ideology—Implications for the Church and Society*. Eugene, OR: Harvest House, 2023.

Simmons, Martha, and Frank A. Thomas. *Preaching with Sacred Fire: An Anthology of African American Sermons 1750 to the Present*. New York: Norton, 2010.

Smith, Kelly Miller. *Social Crisis Preaching: The Lyman Beecher Lectures*. New Haven: Yale University Press, 1983.

Smithsonian. "Emmett Till's Death Inspired a Movement." National Museum of African American History and Culture. https://nmaahc.si.edu/explore/stories/emmett-tills-death-inspired-movement.

Spooney, Robert M. "'Freedom Schools' Key to Primary Goal of Teaching African American History." *Capital Outlook*, Feb. 9, 2024. https://capitaloutlook.com/freedom-schools-key-to-primary-goal-of-teaching-african-american-history/.

Stanford University. "Powell, Adam Clayton, Jr." Martin Luther King Jr. Research and Education Institute. https://kinginstitute.stanford.edu/powell-adam-clayton-jr.

———. "Steele, Charles Kenzie." Martin Luther King Jr. Research and Education Institute. https://kinginstitute.stanford.edu/steele-charles-kenzie.

Swinton, John., and Harriet Mowat. *Practical Theology and Qualitative Research.* United Kingdom: SCM, 2016. Kindle.

Taylor, Barbara Brown. *Holy Envy: Finding God in the Faith of Others.* New York: HarperOne, 2019.

Terrell, Mary Church. "The Lynching from a Negro's Point of View." *North American Review* 178.571 (1904) 853–68. https://www.jstor.org/stable/25150991.

Thomas, Frank A. *Introduction to the Practice of African American Preaching.* Nashville: Abingdon, 2016.

———. *They Like to Never Quit Praisin' God: The Role of Celebration in Preaching.* Cleveland, OH: United Church, 1997.

Thompson, Lisa L. *Ingenuity: Preaching as an Outsider.* Nashville: Abingdon, 2018.

Tisdale, Leonora Tubbs. *Prophetic Preaching: A Pastoral Approach.* Louisville: Westminster John Knox, 2010.

Vogels, Emily A., et al. "Americans and 'Cancel Culture': Where Some See Calls for Accountability, Others See Censorship, Punishment." Pew Research Center, May 19, 2021. https://www.pewresearch.org/internet/2021/05/19/americans-and-cancel-culture-where-some-see-calls-for-accountability-others-see-censorship-punishment/.

Volf, Miroslav. "Shopkeeper's Gold." In *Against the Tide: Love in a Time of Petty Dreams and Persisting Enmities*, 137–39. Grand Rapids: Eerdmans, 2010.

Walker, Wyatt T. *Somebody's Calling My Name: Black Sacred Music and Social Change.* Valley Forge, PA: Judson, 1979.

Warren, Louis Austin. *Lincoln's Youth: Indiana Years, Seven to Twenty-One, 1816–1830.* New York: Appleton-Century-Crofts, 1959.

Warren, Sylvia L., and Carl MaultsBy. "Alumni Updates: Remembering the Rev. Canon Nelson W. Pinder, '59." https://issuu.com/nashotahlibrary/docs/the_missioner-fall_2022-digital-issuu/s/16771752.

Watson, Lea. "Anti-DEI Efforts Are the Latest Attack on Racial Equity and Free Speech." ACLU, Feb. 14, 2024. https://www.aclu.org/news/free-speech/anti-dei-efforts-are-the-latest-attack-on-racial-equity-and-free-speech.

Whitehead, Colson. *The Underground Railroad: A Novel.* New York: Knopf Doubleday, 2016.

Williams, Hyveth. "Preaching Social Justice." *Faculty Publications* 4173 (2021) 19–23. https://digitalcommons.andrews.edu/cgi/viewcontent.cgi?article=5216&context=pubs.

Wimbush, Vincent L., and Rosamond C. Rodman. *African Americans and the Bible: Sacred Texts and Social Textures.* New York: Continuum, 2000.

Woodson, Carter G. *The Education of the Negro Prior to 1861.* New York: Knickerbocker, 1915.

Zinn Education Project. "Nov. 2, 1920: The Ocoee Massacre." https://www.zinnedproject.org/news/tdih/ocoee-massacre/.

www.ingramcontent.com/pod-product-compliance
Lightning Source LLC
LaVergne TN
LVHW010104110826
845155LV00028B/474

* 9 7 9 8 3 8 5 2 2 8 7 7 5 *